PAPER AIRPLANE

WEIRD ORIGAMI

PROF. R V M. CHOKKALINGAM

Dedication

As a paper airplane aficionado, I humbly dedicate this book to worldwide community of paper airplane designers and aviation enthusiasts.

Contents

CHAPTER ONE

Introduction

Paper airplane philosophy is known as aerogami, a branch of origami, whose objective focuses on flying paper aircraft. Origami is a fundamentally mathematical form of art, in which one must obey the geometric rules of paper. The book opens with a fascinating primer on the origami to precisely execute folds and creases – a multisensory hands-on activity. Paper airplane is the ultimate symbol epitome, and prototype. The book details the challenges of designing a new paper airplane that is exciting, but daunting. Origami paper airplane always reminds us of Alladin's magic carpet. The book allows the readers to find immense pleasure in appreciating the same sheet of paper over and over again, accepting the same challenge of folding a new paper airplane, and folding that there is always a new solution. To transform a two-dimensional piece of paper into a three-dimensional flying model is not only magical, but also unique exercise in spatial reasoning. The book, nevertheless, illustrates about physics that is associated with every part of a paper airplane from its formation to its flight.

It is true that the paper folding craft of origami enjoys a long and celebrated history in our culture. In Japan ' kami hikoki'- making paper airplane is seen as a hobby for all.

Who has not built a paper airplane and experienced the joy and frustration of such a simple toy. Let us not overlook the simple joys that can be found in designing, folding, and flying the simple flyer. When we see how a single piece of folded paper can fly in the air, it will inspire us to make things with our own hands and to explore. To the questions like how far can we make fly? And how long we can make to stay in the air? the answer depends partly upon the size and type of paper we use. Our paper airplanes have to be thought of, then designed, and then folding it the right way. We have to keep the wings level, strive for smooth acceleration, and hold it where the most layers for a fast throw. We need to explore the concept of stability while making and flying a simple paper airplane. We can make a paper airplane design for nearly every possible purpose. No engine, just A4 sheet and a pilot throwing it is enough to earn a world title.

The most commonly accepted definition of origami is paper folds that use no cuts, or glue. Many paper airplanes are origami based, which imposes extra limits on the paper airplane with no cuts or glue. There are plenty of examples of paper airplane to start with a rectangular sheet of paper with folds happen too create a streamlined form. With a stretch of imagination, one could easily include the making of paper airplanes in the term origami. When we throw a paper airplane, it will glide gracefully through the air, and smoothly come to land on the ground after running out of energy from the initial thrust. Gliders are typically easier to fold than traditional paper airplanes with its relatively long wingspan, and narrow body shape. Washi paper in Japan is recognized as a sheet of thin foil glued to a sheet of thin paper, which is made to be tougher than ordinary paper. Professional paper airplanes are made out of 60 gsm A4 (8.5x11) paper used in photocopy machine or printer.

The greatest thing about paper airplane is that it allows us to be creative, and that paper is easily accessible. Newspaper is most likely the most produced paper product in the world, but few paper airplanes are made of it. We can use any type of paper, like the news paper, which allows us to try lots of things, see what happens to the paper airplane, and watch science fly. There are a few secrets to making paper airplane that flies well. We tend to focus on the folding pattern and throw, but what we often overlook is the fine-tuning adjustments. When we bend the back edge of the wing up little bit, this prevents nose dive. We need to pitch the back edge between our fingertips and bend upward to create a small flap. The wing tips must be higher than the middle of the airplane, which is called dihedral, which keeps the paper airplane fly better. We can try different size wingtips or try angling the wingtips more, or try different flap settings or different throwing angles. It is also important to keep paper airplane from unfolding, and all the creases must be sharp to hold together.

Making paper airplanes is an awesome classic activity for kids. Kids start attempting to fold them themselves and they actually doing a really great job. Once they have their paper airplanes folded, they let them fly. They fly the planes through the air testing whose plane can go the farthest, highest, furthest, or short distance. Sometimes they try to see if the plane can do tricks, like loops, and spins. Sometimes they hold the plane in their hands and run around making airplane noise. The skills that kids develop while making paper airplanes are: creativity, how to follow instructions, problem solving, and basic understanding of the forces of flight. Making paper airplanes can be an extremely creative process, from picking the colour of the paper, and which type and style of paper airplane to fold. Trouble shooting the paper airplane's fold or flight is a great lesson in problem solving for kids. Finally, the kids will learn about the four forces of flight: thrust, drag, lift, and gravity. They also learn how to throw the paper airplanes to use a light grip, a quick throw, and release when the hand is level with the ground.

Paper airplanes have been as much a part of our dream of flying. Many among us have taken this up further into lifelong hobby. There are paper airplane websites that offer free printable downloads of various paper airplane styles. The styles range from basic design, intermediate, to advanced, and even have a couple of novelty designs to try out. The best part of other than the printable guidelines is the tutorial videos for each design showing us how to construct them, which is perfect for the paper airplane amateurs, kids, and adults alike. They also give us a bit of extra creative flexibility using different colours and paper types. Besides folding paper airplanes, we have to think about the best way to launch them. Many competitions are held around the world to see who can make the best one. The judges in paper airplane competition look for three things: the construction, the creativity, and the flight performance. It is amazing to see some of the contestants come up with sensational ideas, we get really fascinated by the creativity on show.

Paper airplane philosophy: A simple idea that has been culturally embraced for thousands of years; flying paper airplanes is an inexpensive, healthy, and stimulating form of entertainment. Today, paper airplanes hold a firm place in the traditional hand-made playthings that kids enjoy the world over. The simple paper Dart has become something of a symbol for paper's versatile nature. A paper airplane can help us more greatly appreciate warm sun and beautiful sky. The paper makers are always eager to celebrate the magic of paper by organizing a paper airplane contest. We can celebrate paper airplanes by teaching our children the art and joy of folding them. We will also have a blast making paper airplanes together and flying them in the sunshine. We can make all kinds of paper airplanes with just ordinary scrap paper for gliding, fast travel, stay aloft, and sending notes. By observing certain flight characteristics of unique designs, we can experiment with some designs of our own. We look at the sky and send them forward: they flutter, fall, and find home in the coffin called earth.

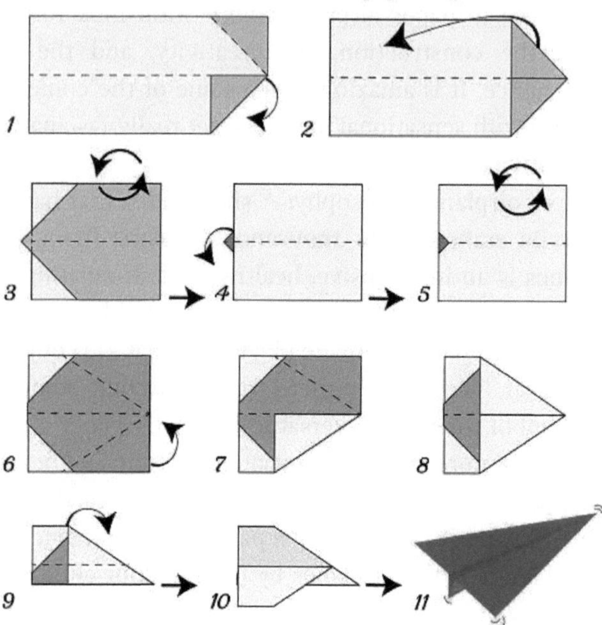
Instructions. How to make a paper airplane
1
2
3
4
5
6
7
8
9
10
11

The Dart

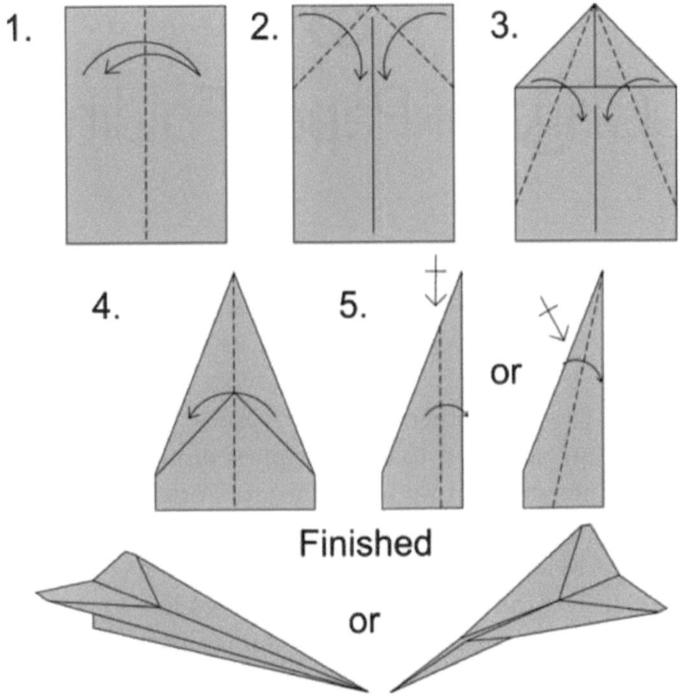

1. 2. 3.

4. 5. or

Finished

or

CHAPTER TWO

Origami Paper Folding

Origami is the Japanese art, or process of folding a single sheet of paper into representational shapes. Everything we want to know about origami is in its name. The word origami from Japanese: ori means to fold and kami means paper. Origami is therefore, the Japanese art of folding paper into shapes. It basically involves turning a piece of paper into an object we want. The art of origami has been practiced in Japan since the 17th century. The art of paper folding is incredibly popular among people all over the world. Over the years, origami has evolved into something more than just an art form. The best thing about origami is that we just need a sheet of paper in order to start pursuing this hobby. The only other thing which we would need in order to pursue this hobby of origami is our creativity and some knowledge about the folds. Origami might seem like a complicated art, but once we know about the folds as well as the way in which the paper can be modelled, the sky is the limit. If we have ever spent a lazy weekend making paper airplanes, we already know the fun of playing with origami.

Origami is considered part of the field of craft and design with many applications, not just artistic, but also scientific. Leonardo da Vinci, one of the first in a long line of inventors, experimented with planes made out of parchment, and of testing some of his early ornithopter, an aircraft that flies by flapping wings, and parachute designs using paper models. Thereafter, George Cayley explored the performance of paper gliders in the late 19th century. The Montgolfier brothers had just casually hung a paper bag up over the wood fire, which led to the discovery of the hot-air-balloon. The most significant use of paper models in aircraft designs were by the Wright brothers between 1899 and 1903. Thus paper has always been a suitable medium for man's dreams of flying like a bird. In 1930 Jack Northrop used paper airplanes as test models for larger aircraft. In recent times, paper model aircraft have gained great sophistication, and very high flight performance far removed from their origami origins. Of course, psychologists find value in a variety of ways to make intricate paper airplane designs.

Origami is about bringing out through folding. A piece of paper is a versatile material for all activities concerned with paper airplane. The properties of paper give the airplane all the attributes it needs. Paper is made of cellular fibres most of them obtained from pulped timber. The slender fibres are flexible enough to bend, and when paper is rolled up they are pushed slightly closer together. However, the resulting curl can be removed by bending that paper back and pressing it out flat. It is only when a sheet of paper is creased or folded that many of the tiny wooden fibres are broken. That is why the crease in paper airplane can never be removed. Paper makes a good wing because it is impermeable to air. In the case of paper airplane, or for the matter any origami, the first thing is to learn the art of folding paper: how, where, and in what way it should be folded. The precise point of folding and flying paper airplane is for amusement, for entertainment, and for joy, because it is fun, easy, and inexpensive. Folding paper airplanes may appear easier than it really is.

Origami involves folding two-dimensional sheets into complex three-dimensional models. Almost everyone will have tried origami at least once while growing up. It is an easy technique to grasp: all we need is a flat sheet of paper. Within minutes that paper is transformed into an incredible model or an airplane. It is possible to fold a sheet of paper to any model without cut or glue. When we properly fold a piece of paper as we would during origami, the plant fibres along the crease are pushed into the plastic region of the paper, causing a fracture point at the actual line of the fold. A practical example of this is, if we were to fold a piece of paper, we will note that if we stretch the paper evenly on both sides of the fold, the paper will tear right on the fold. The fold then becomes an irreversible structural failure and the fibres in the paper will never regain their original state. And no matter how hard we try to flatten out the fold it will never return to its original state. This is why origami models continually retain their shape. Though origami is generally considered an art, it has evolved into a multi-disciplinary subject.

Origami is widely known as paper magic, which comprises the transformation of paper. We can fold lots of origami from plain copier pare, and coloured copy paper. Literally any kind of paper can be used, and for special projects we search for special, often more expensive paper. We may do origami in solitude, or with a few friends, but it is extremely giving to be inspired by and learning directly from other people. It is the transformation into anything imaginable from a simple sheet of paper without the use of staples. The unique thing about origami is that it can be folded multiple times without getting torn. Generally origami paper is coloured on a single side, and white on the other side. Crease is the line, which is induced on the paper due to fold. Paper should always be folded on a hard and flat surface, and the folds should be as straight and precise as possible, with all corners and edges meeting evenly. Normal copy paper with weights of 70-90 grams per square meter can be used for simple folds. Origami is a very inexpensive hobby if we want to stay with printer paper.

Origami paper is thin, strong, and holds a crease very well. The crease patterns in origami are a quick and an easy way to record how to fold an origami model. Creases are the lines on a piece of paper when we unfold an origami model. A crease pattern is basically just an origami model, for example, a paper airplane, that has been folded and shows all the creases on the original flat piece of paper. It is much harder to fold back an origami model from a crease pattern than it is from a diagram. Origami crease patterns serve many purposes to the designer, particularly, they can provide signpost on the way to fold. In a crease pattern we can see everything that is hidden in the folded work. Sometimes it can be a mystery. Origami crease patterns are heavily influenced by flat-foldable rules. Another very important aspect of crease patterns is that it is a blueprint of a base, not of a model itself. To the everyday viewer, they can provide an alternative way of looking at folded subject. Most folders including me prefer to work with regular A4 size copy paper.

Origami transforms the potential of a piece of paper without changing its volume and weight. It is a hobby that anyone can pick up, and suitable for all ages, and all we need is a single sheet of paper. Learning the basic origami folding techniques will allow us to master any type of origami design with a little practice and patience. All origami designs start with the same basic folds which we have to practice- simply fold the paper in half along the vertical, horizontal, and diagonal axis. There are a variety of folding techniques, which come under the art of origami. Indulging into paper crafts is one of the best ways to exhibit our creativity. The basic number of folds in origami creation is small. But they can be combined in countless ways to create everything including paper airplanes. We need to look for the symmetry in the folds as it is a big part of the beauty and appeal of origami. Every crease needs to be flattened for a stable model. We can reinforce a crease by running the side of our thumbnail along the fold, or by using a plastic ruler. We have to strive for that perfect geometric shape as we squash.

Origami is a fun way to explain physics concepts. A vast array of origami patterns can be applied to the folding of near-zero thickness such as paper. Everyone loves origami and are enamoured with their first paper airplane. A small number of basic origami folds can be combined in a variety of ways to make intricate paper airplane designs. If we take an origami model of a paper airplane, for example, and carefully unfold it, we will see the pattern of creases that act as a blueprint for the model. There is some innate component of human nature that drives the basic interplay of mind, fingers, and paper. Origami, the ancient art of paper folding, has applications in the modern-day classroom for teaching geometry, fractions, and fun science. Folding paper can demonstrate the fractions in a tactile way. Nowadays, origami paper aircraft has gained many new and exciting designs over the years, gained much in terms of flight performance. We have to adopt the educational philosophy of finding teachable moments in everything, which includes paper airplanes too.

Origami has the characteristics of a game: it is an enjoyable activity; it follows certain rules; it involves emotions; and it teaches through doing. There is nothing like the timeless pleasure of a paper airplane. Paper airplanes allow us to easily enjoy creating multiple models of paper aircrafts and can take any shape or form we like. People might have thought of paper airplanes as little more than simple toys and ways to annoy our classroom teachers. Most often paper airplanes make appearance only when the designer has idle time on his hands. Each one of us has had a try at one time or another; using paper from school exercise books or pages torn out of glossy magazines, clumsily, or carefully folded. They are around for a good reason and continue to play a part in people's lives today. There is the tale of a well-known professor who made a paper airplane out of the program during a boring evening at the theatre, involuntarily let it fly, and immediately it attracted more attention than the action on the stage. Paper airplane making and flying is so popular among cultures.

Origami engages and enhances skills associated with improved spatial perception and logical sequential thinking. It has been a rite of passage for many young boys to be able to make paper airplanes that can stay in the air and fly longer and farther than all of their friends' paper airplanes. There is actually a great deal of science that goes into paper airplane making and there are paper airplane guys around the world who continually experiment with paper airplanes, trying to get them to fly farther, faster, and better than ever before. Countless paper airplanes have flown through the air to make their first smooth or sometimes rough landing. Many prototypes possibly make an untimely landing in the waste paper basket, but persevere. It is no surprise that the little shapes of folded paper airplanes are one of the least understood and most abused models in education. In most classrooms they have been a disciplinary problem and challenge rather than an educational device or opportunity. Kids always enjoy creating paper airplanes, throwing them to the air and watching as they fly mid-air.

Origami has been found to strengthen an understanding of geometric concepts, formulas, and making them alive. Despite today's digital world where kids spend most of their time on screen, paper airplanes remain the easiest and most enjoyable toy aircraft to build and fly. Just one sheet of paper can lead to a whole lot of fun. All we have to know is how to fold and we can have a simple paper airplane in a matter of minutes. There is lot of cool science in this paper airplane, such as how the different forces allow a paper airplane to fly. Paper airplanes are fun and easy to make. Watching paper airplane floating and gliding in the air gives us a very satisfying and happy feeling. What allows the paper airplane to glide through the air and why does a paper airplane finally land when it is flying, the four forces of thrust, lift, drag, and weight are acting upon the plane, affecting how well its journey through the air goes. There are hobbyists who all engage in the part-time of creating complex paper airplanes that can reach amazing distances with surprising stability.

Origami paper folding is at once instructive and attractive, which appeals to the creative, inventive, and constructive abilities of each and everyone. Paper folding is a multi-sensory hands-on activity, which improves multiple cognitive skills. Symmetry, proportion, angle, bisection, and a variety of other math concepts can be taught with origami. It may also be fun and enjoyable to perform research and practice folding and, making the perfect paper airplanes. There are a lot of tips and tricks to learn about that will help anyone to increase their ability to build a paper airplane that will look remarkable and fly great distances. Learning how to make a paper airplane is a great way for everyone to learn about shapes and symmetry, while also developing fine motor skills and eye-hand coordination. However, when we take a regular piece of paper and try to make it fly for the first time, it will flutter, tumble, flip around in the air and do all sorts of crazy motions. The paper airplane when thrown, will travel in a different path each time as it is affected by wind speed and direction.

Origami helps us to construct the concept of first-things-first, and follows the sequence of steps. There are three basic folds we need to learn to begin folding simple origami models. The most basic of all origami folds is the valley fold-it makes the paper sink down and is indicated with dashed lines. The mountain fold is essentially a valley fold in reverse- it makes the paper rise up like a mountain and is indicated by a line made of dashes and dots. The squash fold is necessarily a neat way of squashing paper into position- it is a compound fold that is to get a feel for the correct placement of the paper during a squash fold. Making a centre crease by folding the paper equally in horizontal, vertical, or diagonal is called crease fold. As it is true with all paper craft, the type of paper we use makes all the difference: a printer paper is ideal for the aerodynamics of a paper airplane. Birds glide and soar in an effortless way, and paper airplanes, when tuned properly, can also glide for long distances. But paper airplanes, while simple to make, involve surprisingly complex aerodynamics.

Origami paper airplane makes the project more individual centred, but also builds our research skills. Some of us fold a traditional paper airplane and then give up when it does not fly as far as desired. We often keep folding the same design over and over again and becoming more and more frustrated because it would not fly. Manipulating the design of paper airplane changes the size and direction of flight forces and those changes make changes in the motion of paper airplane. We need to design and build our own paper airplanes keeping in mind the four forces affecting its flight. The design of any paper airplane plays a vital role in its performance, and also decides whether it is a glider or dart or a stunt one. The most amazing thing about paper airplane is that we need to make one is a sheer sheet of paper. It can be made and used by all age groups and it is a fascinating hobby. Most paper airplanes have just a wing and fold of paper on the bottom that we hold, when we throw the plane. A paper airplane has no motor, but instead relies on gravity for its gliding movement, much like a gliding bird.

Origami fold states, such as the unfolded and flatten-folded states, have geared interest in the artistic and mathematical fields. Of course, there is no good mathematical model for predicting the seemingly simple, but subtle gliding flight. A key criterion of a successful glider is that the centre of mass must be in the just right place. The researchers have found that the flight motions depend sensitively on the centre of mass location. There is a sweet spot for the centre of mass that gives stable gliding. For us at home, the paper airplane continues to serve as a model to explore physics, aerodynamics, and engineering. A small dent or fold in a symmetrical paper airplane can lead to disturbing its course of direction, sometimes stopping them even from flying. There are various ways to fold paper airplanes and each may have different flights. A paper airplane that has balance of lift, thrust, gravity, and drag will fly longer, while a paper airplane with little or no balance will have shorter flights or may possibly nose dive straight to the floor. Always the paper airplane movement comes from the force of the throw.

Origami is stimulating innovation in science. The air around us is one thing that helps a paper airplane flying. When we move our hands through the air, we are able to feel the air on and around our hands. Different paper airplane designs put the four forces to work differently. Darts, for instance, use a strong thrust, as such it is sure to throw them hard. Glider-types on the other hand, float without much thrust, but have a lot of lift. It may sound simple, but many important design choices contribute to successfully keeping a paper airplane in the air. Weight pulls the paper airplane down, lift pulls the paper airplane up, thrust moves the paper airplane forward, and drag pulls the paper airplane back. The aerodynamics of paper airplane will need to have little drag and be light enough to defy gravity. Long-distance paper airplanes are usually thrown at a very high speed to reach more distance. For a paper airplane to stay afloat in the air for a longer time, we need to have its wings wider, and we will require minimal thrust to launch it.

Origami paper is the most critical part of the paper airplane. Here are several properties that can vary between different types and brands of paper. Understanding these properties and how they change the paper airplane's aerodynamics is essential in designing and building good paper airplanes. The important paper properties include: strength, stiffness, stretch, weight, and texture. All of these properties have an effect on the actual folding of the paper. But when it comes to flying paper airplanes, the three important properties are weight, texture, and stiffness. The paper should not be too stiff for folding, and stiff paper wings would not curve due to the difference in air pressure on the top and bottom of the wing. This may cause decrease in lift, and increase in drag, thereby, shortening paper airplane flight time. The lighter stock may show a little instability if not well trimmed. The texture of nice looking paper available can cause a bit of extra drag. So, it is the final view of many professional paper airplane guys that the best paper is plain paper and also copier paper.

Origami is usually connected to fun and games, but it has grown in many aspects-mathematical, scientific, artistic, or even enjoyable craft. While origami can be simple and fun for children, the application of origami in the sciences has been sophisticated and complex. Origami helps in the study of mathematics and science in many ways. With origami it is possible to create large structure that fold up for transportation, or for squeezing into tiny space. Computational algorithms are used by origami artist to create higher complex representation of birds, planes, and insects. Innumerable variations of shapes can be created with only one sheet of paper through origami, which is stimulating innovation in science. Origami offers patterns in creating efficient and flexible structures. Scientists and engineers have begun investigating the surprisingly rich mathematics underlying origami. The art of origami, a paper folding art is deciding technological and artistic applications and even space flight. The creativity and beauty in origami seem to enter the real of science.

Origami is a popular hobby world over both for children and adults. Origami as a hobby improves better eye-hand coordination, attention to detail, sequencing capability, and mathematical reasoning. The art of folding paper helps in improving our problem-solving skills by assisting people to determine more than just a single solution to an issue. Origami promises several therapeutic benefits and helps trigger a sense of belonging. Origami helps instil in us a sense of fulfilment, happiness, and achievement for completing a task. It assists kids with contemplating pictures, visuals, theoretical, and shape. Once we start to know the folds by heart, it will end up being a thoughtful procedure that enables us to persistence. All we need to do is learn the basics of origami, and we will be good to go with it. For stunning origami model, we can think of using some creative hobby ideas with paper. Nowadays, the Internet is abundant with diagrams and videos of a huge variety of models for free, besides origami books. Computational origami explains the way three-dimensional origami structure can be created.

Origami is the first art of using three-dimensions and requires skilful hands to make objects out of paper. Origami techniques can be used to create architectural designs, and create patterns, playing with light and shadows. Origami is being used to solve vexing design problems, often to fit big things into small spaces. Origami artists are to create higher complex representations of birds, planes, and insects. Origami crease map gives a dynamic elegance with mathematical properties. Origami forms a way of expression for most people especially kids and teens. Origami can be a great exercise for senior citizens, and it could help them exercise their brain and even relieve stress. It is one of the best crafts for seniors, as it engages both the mind and hands. Origami lets the inner feeling and creativity of the person flow, and focus better. This paper folding skill is a must-try for everyone, and has benefits for children in the modern-day classroom. Origami helps students to simplify the concepts of physics by understanding 3D comprehension and theories.

Origami folding is fun, engaging, and constructive. Even toddlers can make a paper airplane and enjoy its simple folding. Origami appeals to those with a meticulous nature. One must have discipline to precisely execute folds and creases. The key to success is to understand and master the basic folding techniques. Even the simplest forms are necessary to be thought over and calculated in every step. The patterns of folds and turns have to be carefully done. When we think of origami, the image of a simple paper airplane comes to mind. Origami creators work with paper only using their imagination and mathematical sense. As origami is an extremely fulfilling hobby, more people are turning to it today. Origami has helped in making creases in everything from steel to sheets of carbon mere atoms thick. From a novel idea of creating basic structures by folding paper, it has become a complex craft that is now passion for many. Regardless of whether we are young or old, we can get started with origami as a form of hobby. It is time for all to get best origami papers and let our mind create magic.

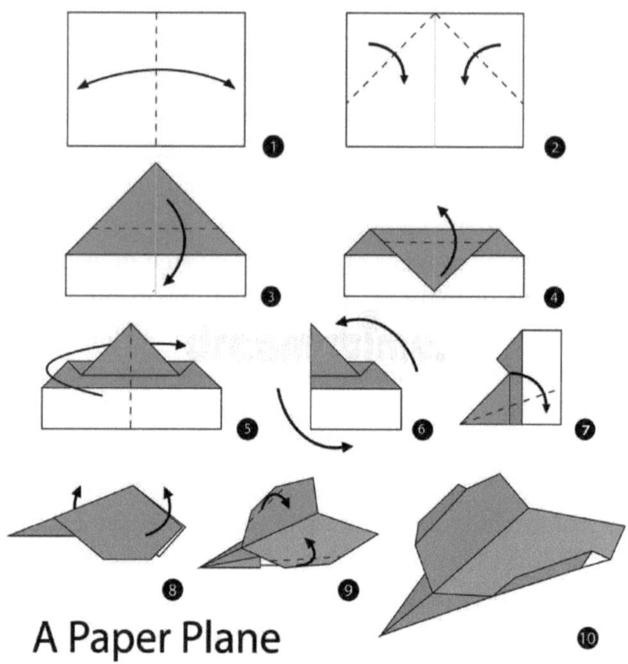
1
2
3
4
5
6
7
8
9
10
A Paper Plane

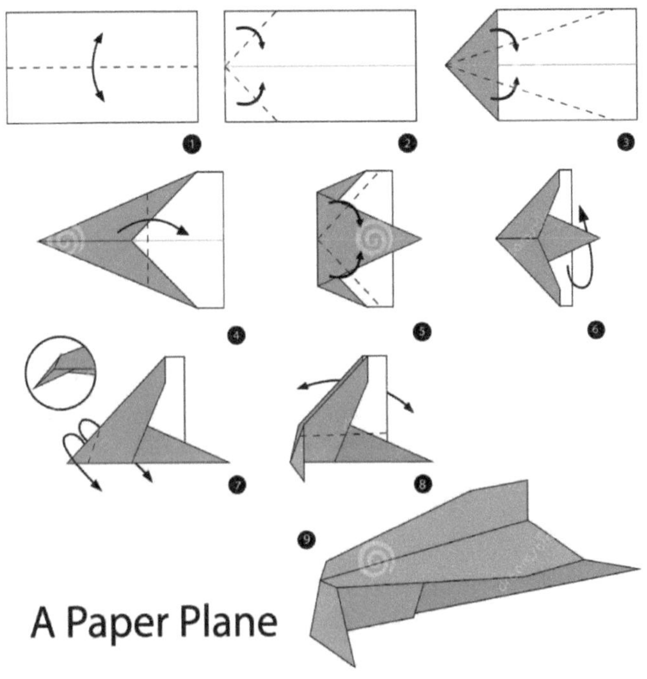
1
2
3
4
5
6
7
8
9
A Paper Plane

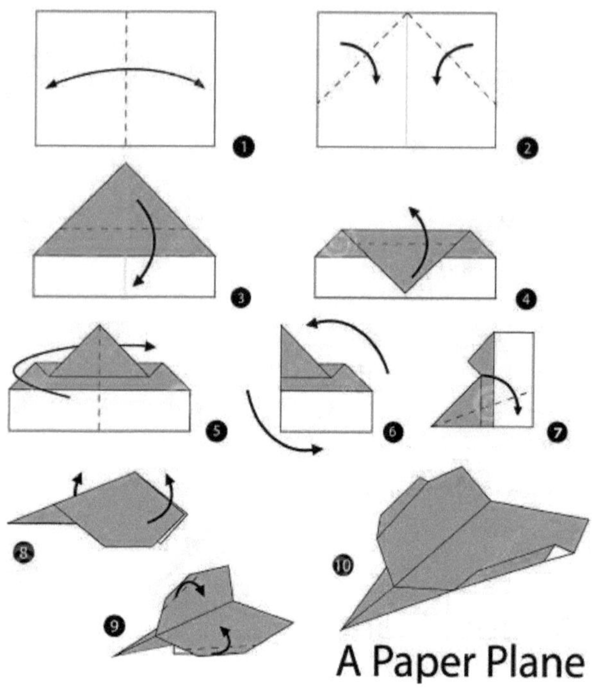
1
2
3
4
5
6
7
8
9
10
A Paper Plane

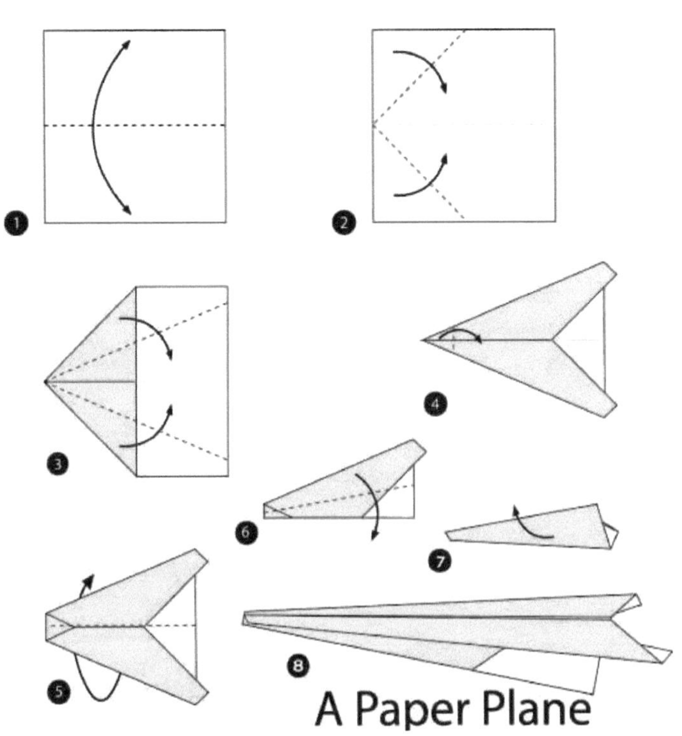
1
2
3
4
6
7
5
8
A Paper Plane

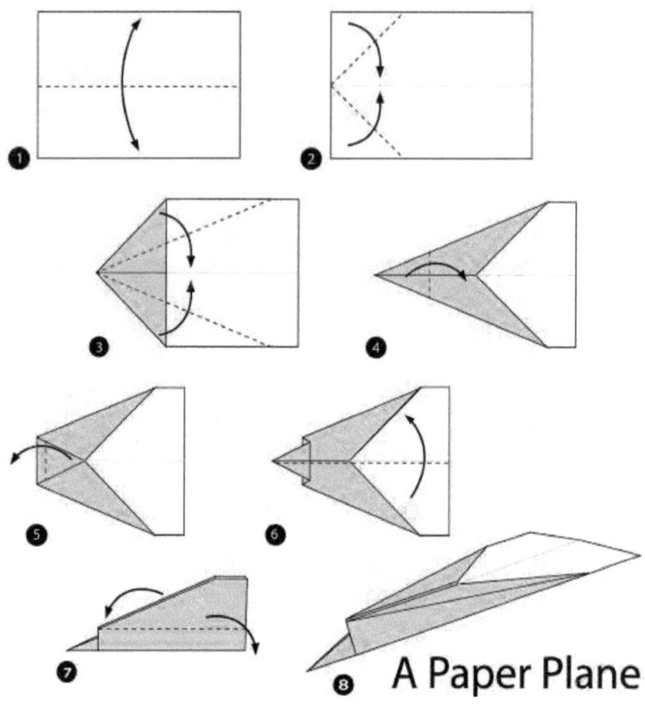
1
2
3
4
5
6
7
8
A Paper Plane

CHAPTER THREE

Aerogami Paper Airplane

Paper airplane is a toy aircraft sometimes referred to as aerogami. Origami paper airplane is otherwise called as aerogami. Origami is simply paper folding, while aerogami is folding paper airplane. Paper airplanes are a classic example of origami in action. The practice of constructing paper airplane is sometimes referred to as aerogami. Origami paper airplanes provide unique and plenty of scope for our imagination to demonstrate high-performance flights. Aerogami is airborne origami. A single piece of paper with origami technique turns into a paper airplane flying over the air. Aerogami is an opportunity to unravel the principles behind design and working of paper airplane. The paper airplane designs have made the best innovation by using origami techniques. There are no cuts or glue considered in aerogami. They are easy to fold, fun to fly, and joy to launch. We can fold exquisite paper airplanes that soar far beyond the basics, using only origami sheet of paper. It is just a challenge to make an aerogami paper airplane and a pleasure to watch it soaring in the air.

Paper airplanes have a noble and storied history that their slender folded frames bespeak. The humble paper airplane has played an important part in man's quest for flight. Evidence points to folded paper gliders being developed and refined concurrently in Ancient China and Japan, sometimes around 500BC. For over a thousand years paper aircraft models were built and studied by the pioneers of powered flight in order to design larger machines. Leonardo da Vince is said to have created his designs for a helicopter, and a parachute using parchment paper. Following the aviation explosion in the early 20th century, paper airplane models remained a valuable testing asset. Paper airplanes are cheap, easy, and awesome. We can create a wide range of styles and shapes from complex designs resembling origami to the most simple paper airplane models. Creative people can develop their most innovative ideas in the unique designs of paper airplanes.

Paper airplane is the ultimate symbol and epitome of imagination. It is believed that the Chinese were the first to build paper airplanes and kites out of papyrus around 2000 years ago. Humans dreamed of flight long before, and have always been fascinated by the perfection of the bird flight. There are cave paintings depicting human flight. In the past centuries many enthusiasts attempted to copy the bird flight. The Greek myth of Daedalus and his son Icarus, is a parable of human flight, which tells that both flew using wings made of wax and feathers, and as Icarus flew too close to the Sun, he met a tragic end. Paper airplanes have captivated imaginations for years with a simple idea: what if we could create something that could fly from a single sheet of paper. Today, paper airplanes are a seemingly universal toy, and even the subject of clubs. The paper is folded in a certain way so that the folded paper actually glides. Paper airplanes can be fun to fly around the house. It is a great prototype-quick and easy. Today, the making of paper airplanes is a hobby and a craft.

Paper airplanes have played a unique and important role in the history of aviation. The fact that birds fly is one of the most amazing things about them. The bird flight is one of the dearest miracles of the natural world, but it is also one that we generally take for granted. Flying birds are beautiful to watch and their incredible feats of agility and speed are truly marvels of nature. Most adaptations a bird has for flight are based on two factors: increased power and decreased weight. Bird flight can be divided into two modes: gliding or soaring flight, and flapping or powered flight. In its simplest expression flying is a balance between two sets of forces: lift and weight, and thrust and drag. Basically bird wings are not flat, but shaped like an aerofoil-concave. Changing the shape of a bird's wing gives it different aerodynamic properties. Flapping flight is basically rowing in the air. Birds are ultimate flying machines and they fly far better than any man-made flying machines. Birds have light-weight feathers, streamlined body, and enlarged breastbone.

Paper airplanes seem to stem from the art of origami. There is nothing like the timeless pleasure of a paper airplane, which allows us to tinker and experience the joy of wonder. Paper airplanes are harmless and require nothing more than ingenuity, patience, and persistence. Making paper airplanes has its recognition as respectable hobby. It is always satisfying for each and everyone to find a paper airplane making gracious flying. Making a paper airplane that will sail through takes more finesse than we might think. Symmetry is very important in many types of paper airplane. Crispy creases help ensure a well constructed plane, and creases in the wings provide greater stability. Many paper airplane designs work best, when they are flown gently. Paper airplanes can fly indoors or out in virtually any conditions. Most of them will fly best indoors, either in a large room or corridor. Even large stairways where they can be launched from the top can make flying areas. We can fly them outdoors too if conditions are calm. By far most paper airplanes bear a far greater resemblance to the fish and the front in particular.

Paper airplanes when tuned properly, can also glide for long distances. Little shapes of folded paper airplanes can go ballistic or make large glide circle or travel a long distance or aerobatic or speedy. Different brands of paper have different properties, but we have to consider what best choices are for successful building and flying paper airplanes. However, the aerodynamic quality of the stock should take precedence. For best flight conditions on paper airplanes, the paper surface should be smooth, but not have a sticky coating. The raw material composition determines to a large extent the quality of paper. Both the appearance and even more so the strength of paper depend largely on the quality of the raw material used. The paper surface structure is an important quality parameter, which considerably affects subsequent performance characteristics. Grammage of paper is defined as the weight per square meter, and expressed in gsm. Thickness of paper is measured in microns, is a significant property related to grammage.

Paper airplanes are a great way to add a little levity to our daily life. There is a simple curiosity about what makes a good paper airplane, and especially what is needed for smooth gliding. It is really a challenge to make a simple fold and fly a paper airplane. Some folds may become quite thick in the later stages of construction, especially when folding the plane in half and folding down the wings, and these will need extra attention. We just need to fold and try a paper airplane ourselves. Smaller is definitely better for a high start. It has been concluded that A4 sheet printer paper is best for folding in order to retain structural stability. Paper airplanes with rectangular design of 8.5 x 11 inches size can have multi-folds at leading and trailing edges. We always try to make a much better one, which is graceful and attractive in the air, or glorious and sweeping glide in the air. For more rewarding is the paper airplane that is carefully folded from a single piece of paper, which glides through the air from the palm of the hand, hovering a while and causing no disturbing noise, and no greasy hands or sticky fingers.

Paper airplanes have been used to demonstrate aerodynamic principles for centuries. To transform a two-dimensional piece of paper into a three-dimensional flying machine is not only magical, but it is unique exercise in spatial reasoning. There is something enchanting about watching our own paper airplane version sail through the air. Traditional paper airplane design, with a few more folds, gives it a more streamlined shape for better performance. There are several reasons to make paper airplanes as an interesting hobby: There is no need to go to the craft-shop, as we need is some A4 copier papers. It is relatively mess-free, as no glue, no cutting, or no glitter. It is a great way to engage our minds in some mathematical, geometric, symmetrical, and spatial thinking. There is nothing more confidence-boosting than creating a paper airplane that actually flies. It gets us running outside to fly our paper airplanes. Aerogami paper airplanes can be classified as acrobatics, distance flown, duration aloft, or fantasy. We need to experiment with each origami paper airplane, and build more effective ones.

Paper airplanes can take sharp edges and points that can injure someone. While flying a paper airplane outdoors, we will be surprised to lose some over the fence, as it is always the best flyers that escape. If there are a few frustrating or finger numbing, folds-that-just-won't-cease moments along the way, then it will only serve to make the end result more satisfying and enjoyable. Yet the majority of them are quite simple to make. All of them can be flown successfully by us as a paper airplane test-pilot. Paper airplanes can curve or change direction after they are launched, so we should make sure our flying area is clear. We should keep in our mind never to fly our craft near moving cars or run into the street after our paper airplane. With constant practice, we can make folding of paper airplane just in a few minutes that can fly graciously. There is something nostalgic about creating one's very own flying paper airplane from a simple piece of paper using nothing more complex than odds of imagination, wit, and creativity.

Paper airplane clubs facilitate children learn how to fold and fly different paper airplanes and launch them. They seek to reawaken a sense of wonder in the craft of paper airplanes, especially among children. Paper airplane clubs inspire them to make things with their own hands and explore with the help of other members. Anyone who loves the craft with paper may join and get hooked with paper airplane club. Paper airplane clubs make children to realize that paper airplanes can be of the easiest hobby to pick up and one of the most entertaining leisure-time activities. Activities like making paper airplanes allow children to spend meaningful time. They help making and flying paper airplanes popular by organizing competitions for best flying paper airplanes. Paper airplane clubs indeed delight several children to fulfil their own dreams of flight and make them feel as their own paper airplanes. They eventually help to promote new folding techniques and arrive at fairly slick designs. A great starting point of making paper airplanes as a hobby, eventually gets back into the rhythm of making high performance ones.

Paper airplanes have been gaining great sophistication and very high flight performance in recent times. Even origami aircraft have been gaining many new and exciting designs over the years, in terms of flight performance. When we start out with folding paper airplanes, it is always good idea to follow the steps to the latter. As we improve our skills, our confidence grows and so we can start being more creative and experiment with new designs of our own. Although paper airplanes have been around for ages, for some reason they have never been adopted for commercial use. It seems that nobody thought of paper airplane in the commercial sense. Paper airplanes are normally seen as a child's hobby, not a suitable activity for adults. This is true even today, though the paper-folding craft enjoys a long and celebrated history in our culture. Aerogami piques our interest in creating some wonderful paper airplanes, but it requires creative folding passion. So let us get ready to start folding: it is a paper airplane folding frenzy.

Paper airplane that is quick and easy to make, and flies far and fast is the Dart. It is called a Dart plane, because we throw it the same way we would like to throw the darts at a dash board. The Dart, also known as simply a paper airplane, is the best known traditional paper airplane design and one of the simplest. Most of us have learnt in our childhood, how to fold the classic Dart paper airplane using a handful of straight folds, even without a prior knowledge of origami. They fly very straight, and quite far as a dart would. Normally this plane is the classic school-yard Dart. We fold A4 copier paper in half way long way, fold the two corners down, bring the slanted edges to the centre line, fold on the long crease, and finally fold the wings down parallel to the back. As its name suggests, the plane's flight is like a dart, straight and fast over a decent amount of time. Dart paper airplanes do not generate a great lift- they are just aerodynamic enough to fly far with a fast launch. It has stiff wings, so it can tolerate fast throwing speeds. We throw it as hard as possible for maximum distance and speed.

Paper airplane philosophy is known as aerogami, a branch of origami, whose objective focuses on flying paper aircraft. When we make a whole fleet of paper airplanes, they bring a lot of joy to us. We can make all kinds of paper airplanes with just ordinary scrap paper- planes for gliding, planes for sending notes, fast planes, planes that will stay in the air for eight or ten seconds. Sometimes the wind will catch on the side of the model and up it goes and it may sail away over the tree tops. We can sometimes have them go over buildings and be lost- much to the delight of the people with whom we make. We also know that it is important to make our folds symmetrical- otherwise the plane would not fly in a straight line. Whatever we do, we need to make sure there is weight in the front of the paper airplane. If it is not, the plane just flutters to the ground as it would if we did not really fold it into much of anything. We probably fold about a hundred paper airplanes, and make adjustments to certain design until we are able to derive the desired looks and flight characteristics.

Paper airplanes can promote technological, yet simplistic innovations. We need to make the most of the opportunity by changing several variables of paper airplane design involving mass to produce the best one. The weight of the paper airplane affects the mass of it. Very heavy paper becomes too heavy and hard to fold. Very light paper like tracing paper leads to too frail. Using paper that is too light will make the plane flimsy and unstable in flight, allowing air gust to knock it off. Using paper that is too heavy will make the plane resistant to wind, and will create more drag in the air, which limits flight distance. A smoother paper surface offers less air resistance, and prolongs flight. Regular printer paper is probably what we reach for when we make a paper airplane. It has ideal thickness to maximize the performance. Building paper airplanes can be a fun exercise in aerodynamics. Normal damage to the paper airplane is damage to the wing, and nose due to repeated crashes. It is a symbolic magic that a worthless piece of paper can now fly.

Paper airplane is where the conscious child will find an irresistible universe. Paper airplane associations hopefully bring fun and enjoyment in learning the principles of flight and provide a persistent drive. They drive the idea that it is economical and fun to build paper airplane models, as they require minimal material of a sheet of paper. Paper airplane associations, however, promote the urge and make this hobby respectable. Making and flying paper airplanes can lead to discussions about aerodynamics. Paper airplane association activities include: presentations to members, scouting events, paper airplane contests, workshops, and motivational programs. They provide good opportunities to enlighten people to develop their childhood hobby into a great profession. It is indeed for the novice paper airplane builder. All they need to get started is unfolded piece of paper and they can get on their way. It can almost a rite of passage for many young children to be able to make paper airplanes, that can stay in the air. Each one resolves to make the plane fly further.

PAPER HELICOPTER

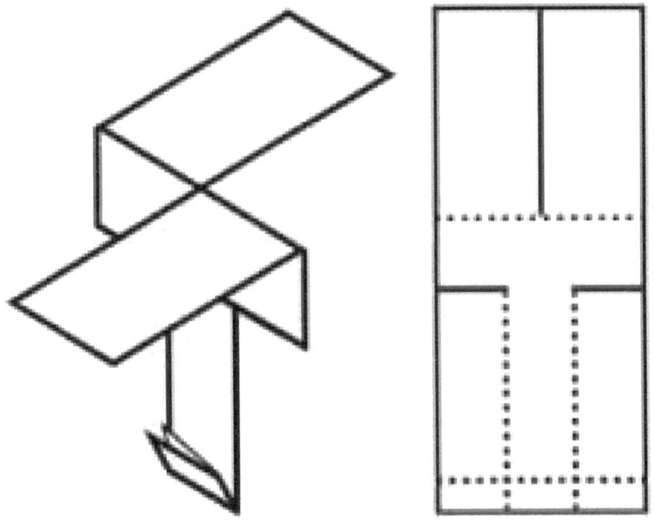

Paper airplane games are those in which children enjoy the competitions. Children need to make at least one paper airplane of their choice and label it. For example, in fly through hoops game, children at a particular distance of say 20 feet, take turns to throw paper airplanes through the rings to accumulate points. In another game, for instance, balloon pop game, each child tapes a pin or a sewing needle, or tack to the tip. Players take in turns throwing the Dart plane at the balloons and attempt to pop them with the attached pin. The player who pops the most balloons at the end is the winner. In yet other game called paper airplane golf, the paper airplane becomes the golf ball, while the paper airplane becomes the golf ball. Everyone starts at the same spot and attempts to get their paper airplane into the bucket or trash can as the hole at a distance. Tracking the number of throws that it takes and the lowest score is the winner. A standard piece of copy paper is used for making paper airplanes for these games. Such paper airplane themed games can be a lot of fun and spice up during celebrations.

Paper airplane always reminds us of Alladin's Carpet. A group of three South Korean youngsters broke the world record for the farthest flight of a paper airplane. Together, the trio achieved the remarkable distance of 77.134 meters or 252 feet 7 inches in Daegu of South Korea on April 16, 2022. Shin who is a paper airplane veteran, formed the trio and folded the powerful paper airplane, while Chee was the designer, and Kim was the one who threw the paper airplanes. A total of eight throws were measured of which this was the farthest. This news was shared by Guinness World Record as an incredible new record for the farthest flight of paper airplane that has been broken in South Korea. The longest flying paper airplane is 29.2

seconds and was achieved by 60-year-old Takuo Toda, in Fukuyama city, Hiroshima, Japan on 19 December 2010. He is the Guinness World Record holder for the longest time flying a paper airplane. And an amazing thing is even today, no one is able to break this world record. Toda is the Japanese origami association president, and a professional engineer.

Paper airplane is a symbol of magic-even worthless piece of paper can now fly. We will hardly come across someone who did not come with paper airplanes. Children, even today, flow paper airplanes to amuse themselves, and often compete with each other. Every one aims to make sure that their paper airplanes soar new heights. Origami means a lot to professional paper airplane guys, and they feel anything is possible and there is always a room to design something new from the same sheet of paper. The accessibility of origami and the varied paper materials that can be used, coupled with the countless designs, they can create such paper airplanes by a lot of trial and error. Designs can vary greatly with an infinite combination of paper type, weight, geometry, and balance. Red Bull Paper Wings is the official paper airplane world championship, under the rules developed by the Paper Aircraft association. The world final is organized at iconic Hangar-7 in Austria in three categories- longest distance, longest airtime, and aerobatics.

Paper airplane means everything to those who strongly believe in magic. We have all folded pieces of paper into plane-like shapes and thrown them at sometime in our lives. With a Dart paper airplane, we have to throw it like a javelin. When we look at the paper airplanes, most of them actually use a Delta Triangle form for their wings. That is something we usually find in very fast jets. Paper airplanes have designs ranging from simple planes for kids to competitive and complex ones for hobbyists. We can experiment with paper airplanes to determine the relation between the designs, type of paper used in the paper airplane and the flight or the distance covered by the paper airplane. External factors such as wind, dust particles cannot be controlled. The tip of the paper airplane must be made straight so that the plane flies smoothly on the basis of its shape and the type of paper. The force of gravity and the drag in the air acting on the paper airplanes are uncontrolled. It is very important to be very precise, when we are folding the paper airplane.

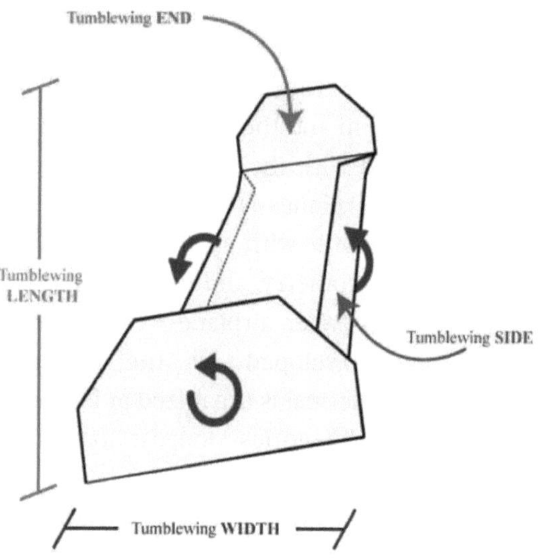

Tumbling Wing

Paper airplane is where the conscious child will find irresistible universe. One of the important factors in designing paper airplanes is the nose of the plane. We need to make sure that we have enough weight at the nose of the paper airplane. Paper airplane has no motor, but instead relies on gravity for its gliding movement, much like a gliding bird. Paper airplane when tuned properly, can glide for long distance. The centre of mass of a paper airplane is the point at which it would balance if suspended from a string at that point. This should be around the middle of the paper airplane. If the centre of mass is too far backwards, the tail of the paper airplane will tend to fall down. If the centre of mass is too forward, the nose will tend to dive down. The ideal location of the centre of mass is slightly forward of the centre of lift. The centre of lift on a paper airplane is the point at which the lift produced by the wings is balanced out. Having a small dihedral angle on a paper airplane will cause it to have a more stable flight, and will help prevent it from spinning. A paper airplane with an anhedral angle may be unstable.

Paper airplane is also very practical and also a great prototype. Origami is fundamentally mathematical form of art, in which one must obey the geometric rules of paper. We appreciate the challenge of designing within this set of rules and engineering each plane to fly in its own particular way. Some planes will fly in a circle back to us, others spiral as they fly, some glide gracefully, and some just fly really far. We enjoy thinking of our paper airplanes as functional sculptures- objects of beauty, not only in their appearance, but also in their flight. It all begins with a sheet of paper with endless possibilities. The challenge of designing a new paper airplane is always exciting, but it is also daunting. We do not cut, or glue, or tape any of our paper airplanes. We find immense pleasure in appreciating the same sheet of paper over and over again, accepting the same challenge of folding a new plane and finding that there is always a new solution. Some paper airplanes are successful, some require many iterations, and some attempts are scrapped entirely. So get ready to start folding: it is a paper folding frenzy.

CHAPTER FOUR

Paper Airplane Physics

The physics of Paper airplane is described by Newton's laws of motion. These laws apply to both the airplane and the air it travels through. The paper airplane is acted upon by a constant gravitational force, and by constant forces with the air, especially drag and lift. It should be stated that there are many different designs of paper airplanes and that different designs could affect the physics applied to it. Air resistance plays a large part in the flight of paper airplanes by limiting the flight distance. When you look at the paper airplane flying, there are a couple of factors that keep it up in the air and going. One is that lift has to be greater than the acceleration down due to gravity. Second is that lift is dependent on thrust with a paper airplane. If the thrust is equal to the air resistance then the object is stationary. The thrust thrown is mainly what gives the paper airplane the long distance flight. To find out the thrust, you need to find the force that you transfer to the paper airplane when you throw it. The paper airplane starts with a flick which gives it its initial velocity.

You do not normally notice the air you are surrounded by. Air has no colour and no smell. Air is a mixture of gases-nitrogen and oxygen. Although these gases are very light they do have weight. Air also takes up space, and therefore has density, although the density is very low. The air is held near the earth's surface by the force of gravity, or in other words by its own weight. Because of this weight, the air exerts a pressure on the earth. Further the air from the earth, the lower the pressure exerted by the air. As altitude increases, the atmosphere becomes progressively thinner; the maximum density, however, occurs at ground level. Since air is fluid, its pressure is transmitted equally in all directions, upwards, sideways, and downwards, including any space to which it can gain entry. But if for some reason, the air pressure on one side of an object is reduced, either the object or the air will have a tendency to be sucked towards the direction of lower pressure. This is the real principle behind winged flight. Winged flight can only function in our atmosphere, which is a comparatively shallow belt of air around.

Paper itself is a versatile material for activities related with basic principles of flight – resistance, drag, and lift. Hold a piece of paper parallel to the floor and drop it. Notice the rate of descent. Wad the paper up and drop it. Notice again the rate of descent. Both fell on the floor, but air slowed down the fall of flat sheet. This simple activity brings the idea of air resistance. Air resistance is a frictional force that air pushes against a moving object. It is also known as drag. Air resistance always tries to slow a moving object down. The faster you move the greater the resistance. When you ride your bicycle fast, you can feel the air pushing back against your face and body. The higher pressure from below pushes the wing of a paper airplane into the air. To demonstrate the force of drag, hold a piece of paper against your chest as run against the wind. You can easily point out the resistance the air provides, which appear as drag acting in the direction opposing that of the motion. A feather or leaf fallen off a tree, gently floats down to the ground.

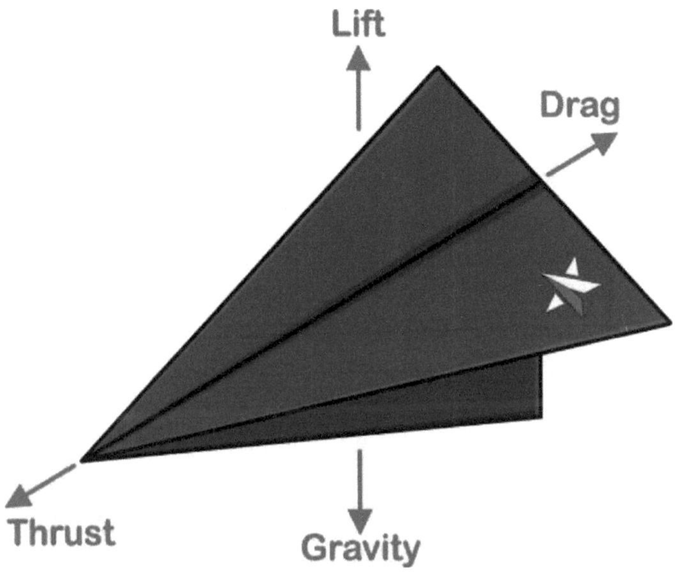

The Bernoulli principle affirms that as the velocity of air increases, the less pressure it exerts. This can be demonstrated quite simply by holding two pieces of angled paper 30mm apart and blowing between them. What happens is that instead of opening up, the two sheets close together. Because the air is incompressible, it has to accelerate to pass through the restriction, thereby reducing the pressure inside. And so the two sheets of paper are forced together by the relatively higher pressure on the outside surfaces. The same principle can otherwise be demonstrated with a piece of paper having 30mm width and 150mm length. Stick the strip to the outer section of a match-box with the folded end near the mouth. Blow strongly across the top surface of paper. The bent paper rises, lifted by the reduced pressure over the top of the paper. The pressure difference between the two surfaces creates the lift. Floating ping pong ball experiment shows that a moving stream of air from the blower keeps a light ping pong ball suspended in mid-air, giving evidence for Bernoulli's equation.

In aerodynamics it makes no difference whether the body is at rest with the air flowing past it, or the body is moving through the still air – it is the relative motion that counts. The forces generated in a stream of air depend on several factors: air density, speed, and the shape, the angle and the area of the surface meeting the air. So, in the strict sense, insects, birds, bats, and aircraft fly, because winged flight depends upon aerodynamic effects, whereby lift is derived from the movement of the body. Paper airplane in flight is in the centre of continuous battle of forces. The conflict of these forces is the key to all manoeuvres performed in the air. To demonstrate the control surface elevator, a simple model can be prepared with a thick sheet of paper, a piece of balsa wood, a pin, and glue. Stick folded thick sheet of paper to one end of the balsa wood strip. Find the point of balance of the whole model and push a pin through at the point horizontally. If blown against this model tail plane, the front of the balsa wood will rise like an aircraft's nose when climbing.

For a plane or bird to fly, its wings must produce enough lift to equal its weight. Most wings used in flight are a special shape-called aerofoil. This shape is needed to help generate lift. You can make a simple demonstration of take-off paper airfoil to show the lift force. Take a rectangular paper of size 150cm wide and 20cm long and fold it over approximately half. Fix the edge by using a sticky tape.

Take care not to crease the paper as you do this. Cut out and stick on a small paper fin near the rear edge of your aerofoil wing. This will keep the wing facing into the airflow when you test it with a sharp pencil. Carefully poke a hole through the top and bottom of the aerofoil wing near the front edge. Push a straw through the holes and glue it in place in the middle. Pass a cotton thread of one meter length through the straw and hold it tight vertically. When you blow air from a fan or hair dryer over the wing aerofoil front, the wing takes off. This is because the shape decreases the air pressure above the wing surface. Planes and birds are both have to be able to provide enough lift force to oppose the weight.

Paper airplanes do not go very far or very high because they use only the weakest elements of thrust and lift, and because there is only so much that you can do with a sheet of paper. A paper airplane flies through the air with a constant drag force, and a constant gravity pushing it down and slowing it. The lift generated can be affected by the angle at which the wing is moving into the flowing air. Air drag is dependent on a few factors such as the density of air, area of the paper airplane, and the drag coefficient. Paper airplanes do not really need tails. However, the angle of the tail has a direct effect to the flight of the paper airplane. If you bend the end of the paper airplane wings up, this would make it fly slower, or bend down it will go faster. Wide wings are good for paper airplanes. All paper airplanes should be flown with plenty of dihedral. There is an ideal size for a paper airplane, and increase or decrease in size is sure to effect the distance it will fly. If a paper airplane is built with care, such important physics concepts can be understood.

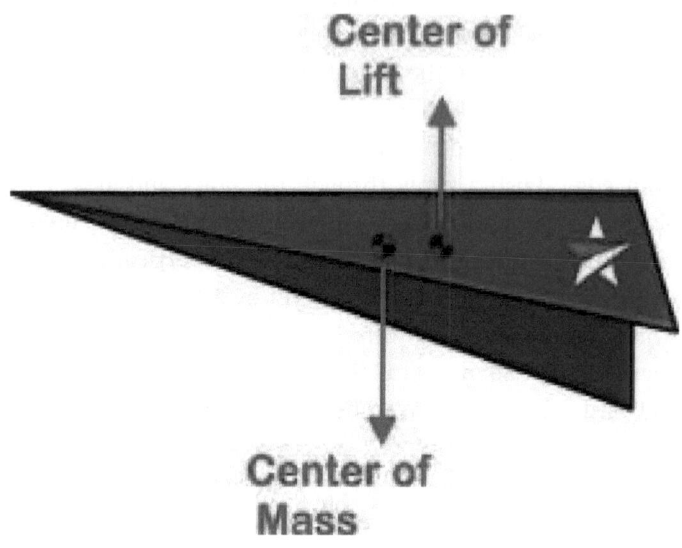

The forces that allow a paper airplane to fly are the same ones that apply to real planes. Real planes get thrust from engines that push them through the air and then lift is generated by the way that air flows over and under the wing. But paper airplanes do not have engines, so thrust is first applied by the launch, and then by gravity. A force is something that pushes or pulls on something else. When you throw a paper airplane in the air, you are giving the plane a push to move forward. That push is a type force called thrust. Thrust and lift are the forces that make a paper airplane fly, while gravity and drag are the forces that will eventually bring it back to earth. Weight of the paper airplane also affects its flight, as gravity pulls it down toward earth. In straight and level flight there is an equilibrium of forces: thrust, lift, drag, and gravity, whereby weight is balanced by lift, and thrust is balanced by drag. For a successful gliding the centre of gravity must remain ahead of the centre of lift- this understanding is very much important.

The more air deflected downwards by a wing, the greater the lift. Generally, all paper airplanes are heavier at the front, causing them to dive and go faster, which in turn creates more lift in the wings. The centre of gravity is kept low so that the aircraft behaves like a pendulum, countering the lateral tilt of the wings. The mass: density ratio of paper airplane influences the performance of aircraft. Thrust keeps the paper airplane moving forward; aerodynamic lift acts on horizontal surface areas that lifts the paper airplane upwards; and gravity counters acts lift; and pulls the plane downward; and air drag counteracts thrust and reduces the plan's forward speed. Once you have made a paper airplane, and given the kinetic energy put into by throwing, this initial throw has dissipated, and paper airplane is glider powered by gravity. The main reason why paper airplanes look different than real planes is to allow the paper airplane constructor to make a plane as easily and quickly as possible. A paper airplane does not need many features of a real one.

Most paper airplanes have just a wing and fold of paper on the bottom that you hold, when you throw it. The distance from wing tip to wing tip is called wing span, and the distance from the front to the back of the wing is called the chord. The ratio of wing span to average chord is called aspect ratio, and is an important characteristic of wings. Low aspect ratio wings are easier to fold, and paper airplanes usually have short stubby wings called low aspect ratio. High aspect ratios reduce drag. The weight forward is good, but a paper airplane needs to have a centre of gravity ahead of the neutral point to be stable. If the centre of gravity is behind the neutral point then it becomes unstable causing nose-dives and spins. Stability means that the plane, if disturbed, will return to its original state. A stable paper airplane tends to oscillate up and down a few times, but converge on a steady flight. Many paper airplanes designs are stable, but just barely. A paper airplane that is unstable will either pitch up into a stall, or nose-dive, but would not settle out anywhere in between.

The combination of the fuselage and wingtips on paper airplanes allows them to have positive directional stability. When you throw a flimsy paper dart across a room, you might not realize that it follows the same laws of flight as a jumbo jet. The key criterion of a successful glider is that the centre of mass must be in the just right place. Good paper airplanes achieve this with the front edge folded over several times. The shifting of the centre of pressure seems to be a unique property of thin flat wings. If the weight is at the centre of the wing, or only displaced somewhat from the middle, it undergoes wild motions, such as fluttering or tumbling. If the weight is displaced too far toward one edge, then the flier quickly dives downwards, and crash in between. However, there is a sweet spot for the centre of mass that gives stable gliding. A paper airplane can get away with just a main wing that gives both lift and stability. Paper airplanes with high wing loads glide faster and have a high rate of descent. A paper airplane with anhedral angle may be unstable and spin as it flies or become acrobatic.

You can discover, recognize, or identify mathematical concepts utilized in folding paper airplanes, such as parallel, perpendicular, angles, and symmetry, etc. You will design paper airplanes with middle symmetry. The paper airplane will not have any curved lines. They must have right, obtuse, and acute angles. There are four aerodynamic forces you encounter in the flight of a paper airplane: thrust, drag, lift, and gravity. There are three governing laws of fluid motion: the first one is just the conservation of mass - stuff cannot disappear; the second one is Newton's second law of motion, which states that mass times acceleration is equal to the total applied force- this is just conservation of momentum; the third one is conservation of energy – the total energy in the system must remain constant. Also a paper airplane will not fly well if it is bulky, or too heavy, or too light, or not balanced, or faulty design, or faulty construction, or front heavy, or back heavy, or does not stay together causing drag or error in launch motion, or uncontrollable variable such as wind speed or wind direction.

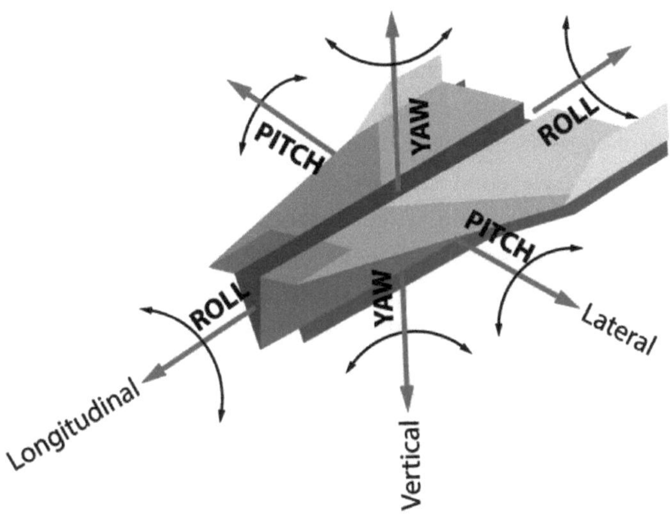

There are many paper airplane designs, and you will notice many of them are not worked well and fly in different ways. It is also difficult to describe fly well or what does it mean to be well. There are numerous designs of paper airplanes with each design being unique in altering its flight. A science project on paper airplanes is to test and conclude the best designs with respect to flight time, distance flown, and accuracy of making. The project also helps you to create your own paper airplane design that is better than the planes that you used in the project. You can find out whether number of folds, affect the distance of flight in the project. You can also work out and analyze what would work best to improve the results of any of the planes. It is also interesting to determine to find out how far a paper airplane goes depending on shape, size, and weight. It is also further useful to determine if adding weight and moving it along the fuselage has effect on its flight distance, and stall height. Thus a paper airplane project will help you find out what is the means of making a perfect airplane.

There are two conditions necessary to make a paper airplane that flies well. It must be able to glide well and it must have good stability. The most important part of a glider is the main wing. A chord line is a straight line drawn from the leading edge of the wing to the trailing edge of the wing. The angle that the chord line makes with the wind direction is called the angle of attack. The angle of attack changes as the nose of paper airplane raises or lowers. When a plane is gliding, wind pressure acts against the wing. This force can be thought of as a vector. It has a vertical component-lift, and a horizontal component-drag. The ratio of these forces is called lift/drag ratio. A paper airplane that flies well will have a high lift/drag ratio. The glide ration is the distance a paper airplane will glide divided by its altitude. The glide ratio has the same value as the lift ratio. A good wing shape is necessary to have a high lift/drag ratio. A good way to do this is to make the wing with a slight bend or camber. The drag of a paper plane can be decreased by making the surfaces of the plane as smooth as possible.

For a glide, a slender wing is preferred. A term that is used when decreasing drag on a wing is aspect ratio. The aspect ratio is found by dividing the wing span by the chord length. The more slender the wing, the higher the aspect ratio will be. In a paper airplane, however, the body of the plane is small, the weight is light, and the speed is slow. Therefore, it is more important to build a light and sturdy main wing with an aspect ratio of about five, or six. The lift/drag ratio changes with the glider's angle of attack. For paper airplanes, a five or six degree angle of attack is best. The weight of the whole paper airplane divided by the surface area of the main wing is called the wing loading. A heavy plane with small wings will have a large wing load. Planes with high wing loads glide faster so that their rate of descent is high. For a paper airplane, if you want a flight of long duration, you need to have a low wing load. You can do this by making a large wing area with a body as light as possible. The paper airplane is essentially a sheet of paper, which is folded in half, which serves as a fuselage.

From experiment, the good performer being the paper airplane made out of regular size 8.5 and 11 inch size printer paper. A4 size paper has a ratio of 1.4, and has an area of 624 square centimetres. Gliders are non-powered planes. They have very long wings to help give them more lift, once they are in the air. The ratio of the length of wings to their width is called aspect ratio. A high aspect ratio indicates long, barrow wings. A low aspect ratio indicates short, wide wings. Generally, high aspect ratio wings give slightly more lift, and enable sustained, endurable flight, while low aspect ratio wings are best for swift manoeuvrability. Long narrow wings give a plane or bird more stability. Long narrow wings also have less induced drag than shorter wider wings. High aspect ratio wings have less induced drag. The less stable wing area means the low aspect ratio wing that is more manoeuvrable than he high aspect ratio wing. A light weight plane with large wings glides well, but travels slowly, while heavier planes with smaller wings travel more quickly and cover larger distances.

Paper airplane has a high potential to be upgraded as a Micro Air Vehicle. Due to its simplicity, paper airplane offers easier design option compared to the biologically inspired designs. Paper airplane offers less weight and cost, which can be fold-based on standard origami technique for any design shape. Paper planes flying in the same Reynolds-number regime as MAV, thus paper airplane has a high potential to be upgraded as MAV. Compared to large flying objects such as light planes, MAVs are also much lighter in weight, normally less than one kilogram, and their Reynold's numbers suggest that they are more easily influenced by flying medium. MAVs can be classified into three main categories like other normal aircraft, namely the flapping wings, rotorcrafts, and fixed wings. A paper plane's gliding speed and rate of descent depends a lot on the wing loading. It would be hard to get a wing load much lower. A smooth surfaced paper airplane, decreases the amount of air, which sticks to the surface of the plane. Birds glide and soar in an effortless way, and paper airplanes, when tuned properly can also glide well.

Paper airplanes are fun to make, but with a few easy tweaks, you can make a special boomerang airplane that will return to you. You can create your own origami super boomerang paper airplane with a few special folds and then launch it with a modified throwing motion. Your completed origami paper boomerang, hold the model at the corner joint with your thumb on top and your index finger on the bottom. Throw up and away from you by twisting your wrist, similar to how you would throw a Frisbee. A paper boomerang is an example of gyroscopic precession. When thrown by grasping at the bottom, it rotates about an axis perpendicular to the plane. The throw gives it angular momentum, which is caused to precession by the fact that the top edge is travelling faster with respect to the air and gets more lift. This produces torque on the spinning boomerang, which continually rotates its axis of spin, changing the heading of the airfoil so that it follows the curved path. Since, it will tend to fly in the direction of the airfoil, the precession causes it to fly in a curved path, and returned.

Paper Frisbees are a common source of entertainment and sport. Paper Frisbees operate on two main physical concepts: aerodynamic lift, and gyroscopic stability. While flying through the air, a paper Frisbee can be viewed as a wing, with Bernoulli's principle governing the magnitude of the lift force, which keeps it aloft. A spinning paper Frisbee can be viewed as a wing in free flight with lift and the angular momentum of the Frisbee providing its stability. The lift force felt by the paper Frisbee is very similar to the lift force on paper airplane wings. The rotation of paper Frisbee is a necessary component in the mechanics of how a Frisbee flies. Without rotation, it would just flutter to the ground like a falling leaf, and fail to produce the long distance. Simply put, the Frisbee pushes air down, and the reactive force pushes the Frisbee up. Spinning the Frisbee when it is thrown or giving it angular momentum, provides it with stability. The moment of the spin also gives its orientation stability, allowing the Frisbee to receive a steady lift from the air as it passes through it.

The physics of how a kite gains lift is very similar to how an paper airplane gains lift. The wings generate lift force by the action of the moving air over the wing surface. A kite also works in the same way. On a windy day, after telling your friend to hold the kite in the direction of the wind, you will give the kite some initial velocity before releasing it. Now, what you need to do is give the kite a little tug to lift it in the air. Running with the kite also helps to create an apparent wind that pushes the kite up. Once released, you do not necessarily need to run to impart velocity to the kite, as the velocity of wind usually increases with increasing altitude, which in turn provides enough lift to keep the kite rising in the air. After the kite has been successfully launched, it will continue to climb into the sky with the help of well-timed, skilled tugs of the string before cruising all at a general altitude. For a kite to cruise, all the forces and torque acting on it should be balanced. When you pull the control string, the velocity of the kite increases slightly, boosting the lift, and making the kite to climb.

Paper airplanes can be found all over the world, and are fun as well as easy and rewarding. A paper airplane can be a simple toy to some, but it is an aeronautics research tool to others. They work as a projectile in physics. Also they help science class to understand the laws of gravity. Math has plenty to do with paper airplanes, such as symmetry, rotation, and stuff like that. Folding paper is analogous to mirroring one half of a plane in a crease. The properties that make a paper airplane fly have much to tell scientists about aerodynamics and flight stability. Paper airplanes can be seen as an educational tool that helps one study aerodynamics and geometry. Paper airplanes can also be used as way to not to trash a paper. Paper airplanes amusement gets you high like a plane into science and mathematics. You can experiment with paper airplanes using scientific method to observe and record. On May 26th each year, National Paper Airplane Day honours the simple aeronautical toy that has been around for thousands of years. In other words, put down your smart phones and get outside for some primitive fun!

CHAPTER FIVE

Paper Airplane Design

The design of a paper airplane affects its flight. A paper airplane cannot fly without wings. The constants of a paper airplane are the folds we make. We normally make a paper airplane of the type we are most familiar with. Paper airplanes are novel creations that just anyone can make. There is no limit on types of paper airplanes and we can invent our own with logical folding. We may get into some frustrated folding, yet it is worth it. Paper airplanes can be made in different sizes, shapes, and paper qualities. We make mistakes and tear off pages from the book. We make a ball out of it and throw it into the garbage. We can make paper airplanes to really make use of those papers. There are many paper airplane designs, some of them are short and pointy, while others are long and pointy. When we flow our paper airplanes outside, we will notice many of them are not worked well, and flow in different ways. We have to make a guess about what might make it fly better. There could be a different method of folding the plane or some other design. We may change whatever we like, but remember to change one thing.

For a traditional paper airplane, a single sheet of paper is symmetrically folded until it resembles a very pointed airplane. The simplest paper airplanes are the flying wing, and that is what most paper airplanes are made. Most paper airplanes have a wing and fold of paper on the bottom that we hold when we throw. Darts are easy to fold paper airplanes and equally easy to fly. Delta wing paper airplanes are triangular wings with extraordinary flying style. Gliders are floaters and continue to fly over long distances. Boomerang airplanes are designed to fly away from the person, who launches it, and returns to him – just like a boomerang. Stunt paper airplanes need tweak in the right way, and can perform loops and camel humps. Awkward and unwieldy flying paper airplanes can be created with crazy designs that possibly achieve flights. Stealth paper airplanes have sleek lines and high speeds, but not easy to fold. Jets and Bombers are paper airplanes that could demonstrate Dig fights, and bomb runs, which are not hard to visualize.

The paper airplane construction is to make a plane as quickly and easily as possible. We can try making paper airplanes out of different types of paper such as printer paper, newspaper, crafts paper, or telephone directory paper. We need to use the same design and size of paper for each, and we will notice one type of paper seems to work best for making paper airplanes, and another type works the worst. Also we can make paper airplanes that are different sizes and compare how well they fly, and for all this we have to make a standard design paper airplane. We have to make our folds as sharp as possible, and if need crease each fold by a ruler. Again we get to build a paper airplane, and change its basic design to see how this affects its flight. If we accumulate a lot of paper at one place depending on the design, it could bring the airplane down. The smaller the paper airplane it goes farther, and the bigger it is, it does not go further. The paper airplane obsession never ends as we start making them, and then we just keep going and going.

The heavier weight of a thicker paper will affect the range of the flight along with different folding characteristics and stiffness. While the thickness of paper affects its flight, the shape of a paper airplane impacts its performance characteristics. We need to make sure that the paper airplane is streamlined. The combination of wing area, and plane weight affects a paper airplane's glide ratio, and range. The launching angle of attack, along with the launching force, will determine range unless there is some outside force. The paper airplanes land safely because of the front pointy. The wing span affects how far, how fast, how high a paper airplane fly. The arrow paper airplane goes farther than any other paper airplane. We can realize that the centre of lift is the point, where all the lifting force can be assumed to be concentrated. We can also visualize that the centre of gravity is the balancing point of our paper airplane: at this point there is just as much mass in front of it as there is behind it. If we put our finger under the centre of gravity, the paper airplane will balance.

The fun of folding and flying paper airplanes, however, needs some useful tips on its construction as well as flying techniques. Pre-flight briefing always helps understanding the little shapes of folded paper airplanes and the fickle ways they display in an amazing way. For a paper airplane to fly evenly, it is essential to check its symmetry. We have to look along the length of the paper airplane, and see if the front-on shape of one wing is a mirror image of the other. If it is not, then carefully shape one of the wings between thumb and fingers to match the other. By incorporating a dihedral, the wings are arranged in a flat 'V', to maintain lateral stability. The way to make sure that the plane flies straight is to check the 'dihedral' of the wings. The dihedral angle is formed by the open 'V' shape created when the outer edge of the wing is higher than the inner edge. We will need to hold the paper airplane with its nose pointing towards us, and look along its length to see this dihedral. The kinks transversal to the air flow may have a detrimental effect on aerodynamics, on the upper side of the wing.

If a draught or gust of wind causes the paper airplane to pitch to one side then the plane will bank in that direction and crash. But if the wings are set with a dihedral, then the wing that drops down has a greater area of lift than the side that goes up, and so the plane raises itself. The aerodynamic forces co-interact, creating turbulence that amplifies small changes in the surface of the paper airplane. Modifications can be made to most paper airplanes by building, curving or making small cuts in the trailing edges of wings. Paper airplanes do not need a tail primarily because they typically have a large thin fuselage which acts to prevent yaw, and wings along entire length prevents pitch. Once we have made all of our folds and the paper airplane looks symmetrical, it is time to trim it or adjust it for flight. If the air resistance is too high, the paper airplane will not go anywhere because it would be like trying to throw it under water. The weight along the wing should be put forward in order to stabilize the plane. We can decorate the paper airplane to give it a personal identity and give it a name.

Trimming of paper airplane consists of slightly bending or warping the ends of the surfaces. When the ends of the wings are bent slightly so that one is up and the other is down, ailerons are introduced and the paper airplane should turn or roll, depending on the degree of warping. When the ends of both wings are up or down, elevators are introduced and the craft should climb or dive. When the end of the fuselage is warped to the right or left, a rudder is introduced, and the craft will turn. The path of untrimmed paper airplane cannot be predicted. When properly trimmed, a variety of manoeuvres can be performed with practice, or straight and level flight can be achieved. The centre of gravity, which can be found by balancing the paper airplane on a finger along two axes, must remain ahead of the centre of lift for a smooth gliding. The low centre of gravity can counteract the lateral tilt of the wings. If the plane banks to the left or right, try raising the rear edge or elevator on the opposite side to the way the plane goes. We can also experiment by bending them down instead up.

Most paper airplanes fly best from a gentle launch, so just push the paper airplane away from us and release. To achieve an ideal long, straight glide the paper airplane may need to be trimmed. Once we have mastered the techniques of folding and flying paper airplane, choose a large room to test fly it. To launch a glider aircraft, hold it up high and level, and just let it go. It will drift slowly to the ground. If we give it a harder push, it may flip over and come flying back towards us. Paper airplanes if built with care, some important aerodynamic concepts can be well visualized. If the paper airplane has a keel, hold there to launch it. If it does not have one, then hold its rear edge between the thumb and first fingers. Of course, the delta-wings with large tail section guarantees stability. A tendency to nose-dive, it can be corrected by bending the trailing edges of the wings upwards. We can give a gentle toss forward to the plane. Our goal needs to be to have it glide smoothly and gently to the ground, either flying straight or in a gradual curve. The most common adjustments are ailerons, elevators, and rudders.

A little bend goes a long way: if the nose rises first and then drops, the paper airplane is stalling. We have to bend down the back of the wing. Always the adjustments are to be kept small. Once we get the paper airplane to balance on the air and float gently, then we can give it faster tosses. We can try lowering the angle of the wing tips to see if we get better performance. Normally, they call for 25 degrees at the wing tips, and we can try a smaller angle and see if the plane flies further. The combination of the fuselage and wing tips on paper airplanes allows them to have positive directional stability without a vertical tail. There are different ways of throwing the paper airplane-right or left hand, eyes closed or open, angle of throwing as well as throwing against or with the wind. Before we throw our paper airplane, we want to make sure we are holding it in the right spot. The best place to hold our paper airplane is more towards the back, just a bit away from the very centre. Holding our paper airplane properly before throwing can make a big difference in flight distance and t

Paper airplanes look different than real planes, because of their exotic shapes, wing design, or no tail. Paper airplanes do not need to fly any slowly so they do not need flaps, or the tail needed to balance the flaps. Making them fly is due to dihedral, weight forward, and wing shape. Most paper airplanes have just a wing and fold of paper on the bottom that we hold, when we throw the plane. Paper airplanes accomplish nose up, and fly slower, or nose-down, and speed up by bending the back edge of the wing up to fly slower or down to fly faster. Paper airplanes typically have a wing aspect ratio that is very high (sail plane), or very low (paper dart), and therefore are in almost all cases flying at velocities far below their wing form. In a single sheet of paper, multiple layers of interlocked fibres prevent air from flowing through. With practicing and mastering the craft, we can make a paper airplane float smoothly even in damp day. Paper airplanes can catch thermals on hot days, for instance, The texture of the paper airplane does affect its flight.

We can make a paper airplane to fly in loop by bending the back of the wings up like ailerons. We have to adjust the wings and shape them in different ways in order to help a paper airplane fly far. The rudder in a paper airplane counteracts adverse yaw caused by the ailerons, when banking for a turn. The larger or the longer the wings are, the more lift it receives, and further it goes. The paper airplane's stay in the air depends on the environment and the design. If we want it to fly farther and longer, we should fold the wings upward. If we want speed, fold them a bit downward. In the right conditions a delta shaped paper airplane flies far. To achieve long flight times, and huge distances, we need to minimize weight-to-wing lift area. Since we start with a simple sheet of paper, we cannot do too much about weight. This, in turn, leaves maximizing the wing area and lift. With its heavy nose and extra vertical stabilizers, the all purpose glider can float smoothly. Based on what we have observed, we need to make the plane that we think will fly the longest.

The mission of a paper airplane is to provide a good time for the pilot, which means the amazement of seeing something radically fly through the air. In the last several years, paper airplane designers have imported techniques from origami. Once we have become proficient in flying paper airplanes, a flight test may be given to trim, which will ascertain our knowledge of different parts of the paper airplane as well as our skill in flying it. We can make flight performance for gliding, rolling, looping, climbing, and landing. Talented individuals can make new and long-forgotten designs: the designs remain unique, varied, and secret. There are more talented paper airplane enthusiasts around the world. We can find some great ideas and good designs for lots of different kinds of paper airplanes. Some are more difficult to make than others. Also individuals who use paper airplanes as a tool of knowledge, experiment with it, and in some cases develop aerodynamic master pieces to fly and study successfully. WE can change the basic design of a paper airplane and see how this affects its flight.

We can introduce to kids how the scientific method can be used to conduct a paper airplane experiment. This paper airplane activity includes scientific method to observe, hypothesis, prediction, and experiment. They are to be provided with several paper airplanes of basic design that vary in size, the person who throws them, and paper weight. These will be thrown to convey ideas about observing, repeated trials in experiments, and the nature of variables. The kids need to work in groups of four, with each performing different tasks during the experiment such as plane thrower, data recorder, measurer, and analyzer. Each group has to be assigned with one of six paper airplane designs, and each representing a particular mode of flying or gliding. All plane flights will be compared to a control design that is designated at the beginning of the experiment. Kids are allowed to throw their paper airplanes more than once, and will discuss the need for replicates, or repeated trials in experiments. Once all groups have conducted their experiments, they are assembled to discuss the results.

Kids are asked to gather for a seminar to discuss the results, and demonstrate how data can be analyzed. Kids will reiterate the concepts of variation, repeated trials, control, and hypothesis- all parts of the scientific method. Scientific methods are steps that are followed during an investigation to make sure that the information gained during the investigation is accurate and true. All the steps such as problem, background research, hypothesis, step-by-step procedure, experimental design, or methodology, data collection, data analysis, and final conclusions. If we want know which paper airplane design is best, we first have to decide what best means of possible. This is known as operational definition. For example, for this investigation, we will define best as the plane that flies farthest. We will not be concerned with height, or loop, or straight flight. Now allow kids a as a group, decide what they would like to test. The length of the plane, the weight of the plane, the sty;e of the plane, position of weights on the plane, or something else.

Now, kids would make a question that states what each group would like to investigate. They find out what is already known about paper airplanes or may use the Internet. Then kids will have to write a hypothesis that states which type of paper airplane that each group is testing. They have to first pick one thing to test out of the ones mentioned earlier and decide what kind of data they will collect as well as what they observe and measure. They can repeat the experiment several times as trials. Then they record the data and analyze the data. They can make a graph or picture of the data and visualize the patterns, trends, and relationships. They now compare recorded flight distances and draw conclusions. The conclusions also discuss the usefulness of the results. They finally communicate results to the experts, compare them to what is already known, and find out what is really true and accurate. Analysis of these experiments with model paper airplanes and their results will reveal new aerodynamic effects that will enable efficient design for farthest flight.

Paper airplane science projects are easy, cheap, and fun. The two problems associated with them are lack of standardization in the throwing procedure, and lack of creativity. It is always a challenge to find a way to standardize the throwing part of the procedure. One has to think about ways to make sure the throw or release is the same each time. We may have to handle variables such as wind or thermals. After we standardize the experimental procedure, we have to decide what we want to manipulate. Quantitative variables we can measure may include Average distance flown 9(length), average time in air (time), average maximum distance from straight line 9(angle from centre line), average additional weight carried a set distance (pay load), precision or degree of variation in between trials, angle and distance from target. In all these things, the more we measure, the more data we will generate. Ultimately, this will translate into a more detailed science project. The science fair project ultimately help us make the perfect paper airplane.

The science fair project can use different strategies: the first one could be we can use the same paper airplane design and the same amount of paper, but vary one of the following namely type of paper, weight of paper, thickness of paper, texture of paper, integrity of paper with or without holes or tears; the second one could be holding all of variables listed above, but vary airplane design with the same type and amount of paper; the third strategy could be we pick one paper airplane design and one type of paper, but vary amount of paper, such that we will have similar style planes out of the same type of paper by varying sizes. Even with a paper airplane science project, we need to become a scientist by asking questions: does the number of folds affect the distance a paper airplane will fly. We can make a working chart including columns on number of folds, and throwing time numbers. We can analyze the data and inform what we guessed, what we have done, which number of folds did the best and final conclusion indicating the result.

Rubber bands could be useful in developing a launch system for paper airplanes. We can build a paper airplane launcher using the concept of a catapult. Using a rubber band launch system, often powered with rubber bands is another way to apply thrust to the plane. We can add a rubber band for slip-shot-style launching. The size of our paper airplane will be dictated by how large a sheet of paper is used, and the length of the rubber band will dictate the strength of initial thrust that sends it flying. We need to make a notched cut at the bottom of the pointed nose at the front of the paper airplane. It is better to wrap a piece of tape around the notch to keep the paper from tearing. Then, we have to place the loop at one end of a rubber band into the notch. Now, we can hold the plane by the bottom in one hand, while holding the free end of the rubber band in other hand. We need to pull the rubber band away from the paper airplane, until it is fully extended. Finally we have to release the paper airplane to propel it forward. Stretching the rubber band turns the elastic potential energy into mechanical energy.

The traditional paper airplane can be empowered with a mini motor. Perhaps, the coolest thing about power-up paper airplane is that it will work with any design of paper airplane. We care to dream up with a single sheet of 8.5 by 11 inch copier paper. As long as the fuselage is big enough to mount the hardware, we are set for action. Dramatically we can extend the loft and distance. The electric power module for paper airplanes is already available, but it does not have the remote control feature. It is a capacitor-driven motor that is only good for about 90 seconds of powered flight. It allows us to mount an electric propeller on our paper airplanes, so they can fly under their own power. The power up electric power module adds propulsion, but no active steering. The recent development in power up paper airplane makes it to look simple- a propeller, a light weight carbon fibre rod, and a battery. It hides an embedded Bluetooth receiver that talks to an app running on our i-phone. We can now just take a piece of copier paper, and turn it into a smart-phone controlled paper airplane.

CHAPTER SIX

Paper Airplane Making

We can make awesome paper airplane design that can fly fast, far, or do crazy stunts. There are countless types of paper airplanes, some inspired by actual planes, others inspiring the creation of planes. Building the perfect paper airplane requires a lot of skill, patience, and precision. Since a sheet of paper is the only building material, it is critical factor, in ensuring our paper airplane is the best, it could be. Paper airplanes are easier craft to make and toss into the air. We not only learn origami, also it adds to our learning basics of aerodynamics of flying them. Some pointers will ensure an attractive and functional paper airplane creation. We need to fold the paper airplane symmetrically, and perfectly. We ought to trim the paper airplane to correct any problem, and toss it at the speed we want it to fly. The centre of gravity should be forward. The heavy front-end design ensures stable flight. A perfectly crafted paper airplane will successfully fly so far so long. If we are patient enough, and keep trying, we will get them right in the end.

The acrobatic paper airplanes are meant for goofy stunts, not distance, and they deliver. The way to perform loops is to tweak the back edge of both wings sharply upwards. When the back edges of the wings are tweaked upwards, the nose of the paper airplane will pitch upwards, when we throw it and it completes a loop. If we want our paper airplane to boomerang back to us, the trick is again tweaks. In order to boomerang our plane in a curve to our left, tweak the back of both rudders slightly leftwards. If we want our paper airplane to do camel humps, we need to tweak the backs of both wings slightly upwards, but only very slightly. The trick here is to tweak the backs of the wings upwards to just the right extent. We will only know the right point, once we have done a lot of test flights with our own paper airplane. For all these stunts to be performed by our paper airplane, we need to use A4 size copier paper. If we want to experiment, we can make some simple modifications to get effective camel humps. Everyone loves those paper airplanes that fly around in crazy loops and dives.

BULLDOG DART paper airplane is simple, and requires a few folds, and flies well. The dart paper airplane is the best known traditional design, which we have been familiar with from childhood. It is called a dart airplane, due to both to its shape and flight pattern. We have to begin with folding the A4 sheet in half lengthwise, and then unfold. Now, we have to fold the top two corners down, so they meet the centre crease. This is the classic way to start a paper airplane. Flip the plane over, and fold the corners in again to the centre crease. The diagonal line coming off the top of the plane to be lined up with the middle both side. Then we have to fold the top point down, so that the tip meets the bottom of where the previous folds come together. Later we need to fold the entire plane in half in on itself. This creates the snub nose, which gives the Bulldog dart its name. Finally we should fold the wings down so that we are making a straight line across from the top of the snub nose. This flies better when thrown at lower speeds.

Let us give it a softer throw.

GLIDER paper airplane is a sail plane, which is simple to build and fly. Position the A4 printer paper horizontally. We have to fold about an inch width from the top edge down. Now diagonally fold down the top left corner, and repeat with the right side. Then we have to diagonally fold down the two new top edges. Then fold the paper in half keeping the folded side up, and fold down the wings with a width of one inch fuselage. Finally we can fold up the wing tips to an inch width. If needed we can curve up the rear edges of the wings between thumb and finger to achieve a smooth glide, by launching it gently. Glider paper airplane is a great way to add a little levity to our mind. In general, a simple paper airplane should be balanced, heavier in the front, having wings and aerodynamically streamline. Luckily, there are a few methods for creating paper gliders that use simple physics to fly with much more grace and ease. The glider paper airplane has broad wings to generate plenty of lift at the expense of speed.

AUTO GYRO Paper airplane, or paper HELICOPTER is really an autogyro, which means self circling. The wings of a paper helicopter superficially resemble the rotor wings of a real helicopter. Its name means screw-wing: a screwing motion that serves as a sort of which aptly describes what happens when gravity-driven paper spinners star to fall. The airflow makes their rotors spin, to delay their descent by providing lift. This simple paper helicopter is very easy to make, and provides a good demonstration of spinning stability and gravity. We need to take a 2 inch by 8 inch piece of paper, and fold it in half length wise. Cut a little less than halfway down the crease that we fold down the length of our paper. Now we have to make small cuts in toward the centre line halfway down the length of the paper. Then we need to fold both of the bottom sections. Finally we should fold top flaps we made when we cut our paper almost halfway down lengthwise. We can drop the paper helicopter, after folding out its wings, from a variety of heights. It behaves like a gyroscope, and its spinning stabilizes the falling paper helicopter.

RING WING paper airplane is a non-spinning glider. This requires only a single sheet of paper, but works best with 8.5 by 11 inch or A4 size printer paper. We have to fold this sheet of paper diagonally, and make a half an inch fold along the previously folded edge. We need to make again a second half an inch fold along the previously folded edge. Now we should curl the ends of the paper to make a ring and tuck one end into the fold of the other. Let us gently grasp the 'V' between the two crown points with our thumb and index finger, and toss the glider lightly forward. When we throw this ring wing paper airplane air rushes into the ring, creating the force of lift that makes it glide through the air. The ring wing files because air flows over and under the paper to create lift. This simple ring wing glider paper airplane is an unusual design that flies with the aid of the 'boundary layer effect' of the air passing over its surface. For this reason, the single ring plane needs to be built correctly and thrown forward by letting it off. It is an amazing ring wing glider, a popular mini glider, and a specific type of glider.

TUMBLE WING glider is one of the most curious paper airplane flying contraptions ever conceived. A tumble wing is a glider or kite wing design, which rotates about an axis traverse to the apparent wind. We can create a tumbling walk along glider from telephone book paper, which lighter and works better. We have to just shear the end of 8.5 by 11 inch printer paper to make a 20cmm by 5cm rectangular strip. We have to fold up one end, then the other end symmetrically with 2cm from each end. We can make a fold in the centre of the trailing edge. It is important that the fold does not disturb the right angle fold that we have created at the ends of the strip. Now we have to turn the strip of the paper upside down, and fold again without disturbing the right angle folds at the ends of the strip. We should hold the folded strip at the centre of the trailing edge with the wing tips pointing up. It is designed to fall steadily forward and down, in a spiral. With the correct size card board, it is much easier to keep the tumble wing aloft. Keeping it in sustained flight is just a matter of practice.

HOOP GLIDER paper airplane is a little different one with an interesting twist. To make our hoop glider we will need two hoops, and two paper strips of 10 inch and 15 inch long and 1 inch width. Now we have to turn our strips into two hoops- one big loop and one smaller loop, by joining the ends together with an overlap of an inch using glue or tape. Then we must attach our loops to the ends of a straw with a tape, in such a way that the drinking straw is lined up on the inside of the loops. In other words, one loop goes at one end of the straw, the other hoop on the opposite end. Now our hoop glider is ready to launch- throw it with the smaller hoop facing forward in the direction of the flight. It may look weird, but we will discover it flies pretty well. When we throw the plane, we are giving it thrust. The big hoop creates drag, which helps keep the straw level. The smaller hoop at the front keeps our hoop glider stable and flying on a straight path. The glider does not turn over since the hoops are heavier than the straw. It may take a little practice, but once we get the hang of it, our hoopsters ill really fly.

BOOMERANG paper airplane is fun to make, but with a few easy tweaks, we can make a special boomerang airplane that will return to us. We can create a special boomerang paper airplane with special folds and then launch it with a modified throwing motion. We have to take normal printer paper, and valley fold the paper lengthwise in half, making a sharp crease and then open the paper. We need to fold two corners to the centre line, making a point on one long end of the paper. Now, let us fold the point down width-wise, so that it looks like an envelope flap. We need to fold the top corners of the paper down so that they meet at the centre line, just above the point of the envelope flap. Next, we should fold the small point of the envelope flap in up direction. Later we must fold the wings so that the edge of the paper lines up with centre line. Now, we need to fold the paper lengthwise in mountain fold direction. Next, we fold the tail flaps up so that the crease lines up with the back edge of the plane. Hold the paper airplane to the side and toss it away from us with banked angle, and see it boomerang back to us.

LOOP paper airplane is amazing as it perform loops upon release. This is due to its design consisting of two flat, wide wings and elevator flaps in the back that make it loop. We start with folding A4 paper in half lengthwise, and make a crease before unfolding it. Position the paper vertically and fold the top two corners downward until the edges meet at the centre crease. Keeping the paper position vertically, we have to fold the triangle down. Again keeping the paper oriented in the same position, fold the top two corners downward to meet in the centre. The two corners will meet about I centimetre above the tip from our previous fold. We now fold up the small triangle of one centimetre up to cover the centre points from our previous fold. Now, fold the paper back in half lengthwise, keeping our previous folds on the outside position of the paper so that the nose is pointing away and fold down the wings. Lastly we have to fold up the elevator flaps on each of the wings to form an isosceles triangle. These elevator flaps pull the nose up causing the loop paper airplane to perform a loop de loop in the air.

TRICK paper airplane can fly for long periods of time, and even do flips. We have to start with folding A4 printer paper in half lengthwise, and unfold the paper the same way we have folded. Now, fold the top two corners to create two triangles that meet at the centre crease. Then we have to fold the top corner to the bottom of the folded part of the paper. Finally, we should fold the wings over by grabbing one side by the outer edge of the diagonal part and following it over toward the middle crease, so that we see a small triangle with a bottom edge that touches the middle crease. We need to turn the paper over and do the same on the other side. This creates a long, rectangular shape with triangles on either side of the plane. We can grasp the trick paper airplane by the hand in the middle and gently throw it upward. We will see that this trick plane creates loops instead of flying straight ahead. It is the best to use plain printer paper for good performance- if we pick paper that is thicker, it will fall too easily, and if we pick thinner paper, it will not be able to gather enough momentum to fly.

GYRO FLYER paper airplane is a cylindrical paper airplane. We lay the 8.5 by 11 inch printer paper landscape or horizontal on a flat surface. We fold the top edge of the paper to the bottom edge, and unfold to create a crease. Now, fold the top edge of the paper to the crease and fold along the crease. Then fold the current top edge to the bottom of the folded part of the paper, in other words, fold the folded part in half. Next, roll the paper, sliding the edge of the left side of the ring into the slot on the inside of the right side of the ring. Finally we can tape it shut along the seam. We can hold it in hand with the thicker edge forward, and toss it like a football, using fingers to give the paper a spin as it is thrown. The gyro flyer uses both aerodynamics and gyroscopic motion to fly. Much like a plane's wing, the front of the gyro flyer is thicker than the back end. This causes the air as it flows over and through the gyro flyer to provide lift, or push it slightly up. The gyroscopic motion is created by the spinning of the tube. Much like a spinning top, it does not fall over.

BARREL ROLL paper airplane completes a full axis rotation. A barrel roll is a spin about a horizontal axis, while flying in the air. One wing turns over the other, and rotates all the way round to return to the stating orientation. To do a barrel roll, we have to one flap up and the other one down in our paper airplane. Ailerons allow the paper airplane to make barrel roll. If the left aileron is down and the right aileron is up; then the paper airplane will do a barrel roll towards the right. If the left aileron is up and the right aileron is down; then the paper airplane will do a barrel roll towards the left. We simply fold A4 sheet vertically in halfway, and unfold. Now fold the left top corner to the centre crease, and repeat it to the right corner. We have to make second fold over the ones already made with the corners meeting at the centre crease. Fold the top corner to the third of length. We can fold the wing on either side with a fuselage. It is now important to fold one wing up and the other one down. When we throw this paper airplane into the air, we will observe a barrel roll flying in a corkscrew trajectory.

BIONIC paper airplane is the simplest way to fold and flies like a bird. We have to position A4 copier paper in a horizontal manner and fold the sheet into halfway vertically, and unfold. Take the top right corner, and fold it to meet at the centre crease. Similarly take the top left corner, and fold it to meet at the centre crease. Now, we have to hold the top corner and fold it down right in such a way it meets the bottom of the already folded one. Similarly, we have to hold the top corner, and fold it down left in such a way it meets the bottom of the already folded one. Now, we get a central fold at the top that has to be squashed in to a square box fold. It is important to hold the central crease in both hands and fold on either side of about a centimetre width along the bottom line. Reverse the sheet and fold winglets of one centimetre width on both the wings. We need to hold the bionic paper airplane at the back between fingers on the top and thumb at the bottom, Hold the plane up and throw it down gently to see the bionic paper airplane flying with flapping wings.

STEALTH paper airplane is a glider plane and it is simple to make one. The stealth is a sweet little paper airplane. This plane is easy to fold and flies straight and smooth. We have to lay the A4 sheet vertically. Fold the top right corner to the left side. Open the sheet back up, and repeat the same step with the left corner. Open the sheet back up and accordion fold sides as normal. Next, we have to fold the right side of the triangle shape to the top point., and repeat with the left side. Now, we need to fold in the bottom right edge of the diamond shape, and repeat with the left. Next, fold down the top point and tuck in the flaps. Gently fold the plane in half away from without crease with partly open. Finally fold out the ends of each wing. The ideal angle between the two wings is around 120 degrees of dihedral for stability. Lightly throw this stealth paper airplane into the air and watch it glide. We can try throwing it from a balcony or other high location to watch it soar for a long time. We can also make a stealth bomber paper airplane with its triangular wings that flies much faster.

BAT paper airplane can be constructed with a little bit of imagination. We start with a rectangular piece of A4 copier paper, and fold in half width wise, and open back up. Now fold each side in towards the centre fold. Next, fold out the sides. Then fold the corners down like we do on a traditional paper airplane. Now, turn over, and fold the top point down to the bottom, and fold the corners down. Fold the point back up, which should cover up the two corners we just folded, and then turn over. We need to fold the point down again and then fold in half width wise. Fold one of the wings down leaving a bit at the bottom to hold on to. Do the same to the other side and we are done. Hold the paper airplane at the bottom dense folded area and just throw it into the air. Bat paper airplane can flap its wings in flight. It is suggested that we use letter paper, as it is essential to use a lighter paper for better performance. Talo Kawasaki folded a fantastic action origami patty bat paper airplane that can flap its wings, and at the same time producing an awesome sounding noise.

WORLD RECORD paper airplane can be folded using A4 printer paper. WE have to start folding the paper in half along the vertical axis and unfold. Now, we fold the top right corner to meet the left edge of the paper and unfold. Fold the top left corner to meet the right edge of the paper and unfold. Fold the left corner to the diagonal crease created in the first step. Fold the right corner to the diagonal crease created in the second step. We have to fold across the horizontal axis, where the two diagonal interior edges intersect. The creases at the top should align with the diagonal interior edges. Fold the top right and top left corners into the centre crease. We need to fold the plane in half backwards along the centre crease. Rotate so that the bottom crease becomes the bottom edge. Fold the left diagonal flush with the bottom corner to create the wing. Repeat with the other side. Now the paper airplane is ready to fly. Tips for optimal flight include: symmetry is key- Hold the paper airplane at the thickest part of the fuselage area with most layers before launch.

There are high-performance paper airplane kits available for paper airplane enthusiasts. Innovative paper airplane kits present a collection of realistic origami paper airplanes. The kits have perfected the art of folding easy paper airplanes that both look great and fly well. The paper airplane designs are also printed in full- colour on both sides, and pre-cut, so we just need to push them out, and assemble them. Although fun for folders of any age, these paper airplane designs are so uncomplicated that they can be considered as origami projects and are great way to learn origami paper airplanes. They range from simple designs that can be constructed in under a minute to detailed scale replicas that look and fly like the real thing. The paper planes can be fired high into the air with a rubber band launcher, and are designed to circle down for a long time. Do-it-yourself record breaking paper airplane kits are incredibly easy to fold and designed to push the envelope in terms of time aloft, and distance travel, exploiting the record breaking paper airplane designs.

Power- up electric paper airplane kits, help convert our paper airplanes into a flying machine. It is an easy to use design with carbon-fibre propeller shaft and ultra-tough rear propeller to make the flight virtually crash-proof.

These modules work with a wide variety of planes, even if our folds are not perfect. Some kits have a unique collection of model paper warplanes from the glory days of the biplane and early mono-wings. The kits include instructional origami book that not only explains how to assemble each plane, but how to fine-tune it to coax the best performance. Also are included helpful tips and suggestions for designing our own origami paper airplane models. We can pick from classic flyers and smooth-sailing gliders to wild rides and looping dare devils. The booklet includes: basic aerodynamics; learn what makes them fly; tips or tricks for great flights; and step-by- step folding instructions for every model. The kits allow us to take to the skies with creative paper airplanes. We can take a hands-on flight through these paper airplane models, just waiting to be assembled.

There is nothing like the timeless pleasure of origami paper airplane making. Beginning with China-the creators of modern paper, and the Japanese-the creators of origami art of paper folding- have winged/hinged on the design of paper airplanes. Paper airplane is the first for children among the many innovative things they learn. Paper airplane is the ultimate symbol and epitome of imagination, creativity, and prototype. Paper airplanes are the best examples of innovative simple toy for the young as well as the old to play with. From Leonardo da Vinci to the Wright Brothers, paper has been truly instrumental to learning how to get objects to fly. Anyone can turn a stack of paper into his or her own private air-force. People can test their paper folding techniques with several examples. More experienced ones can tackle folding designs for specific flight outcomes. Origami crease maps give a dynamic elegance with mathematical properties. We are all fascinated with paper airplanes, and this fascination can be a doorway to rich science learning.

Paper airplane has a high potential to be upgraded as a Micro Air Vehicle, due to its simplicity. Paper airplanes offer easier design options compared to the biological inspired design. Researchers, however, have underestimated and overlooked the basic aerodynamic performance induced by the paper airplanes. This is again due to its common usage as toys and a wide range of paper airplane design. They can analyze and compare the aerodynamic forces, and its performance for selected paper airplane designs known as glider, dart, or stunt. The properties that make a paper airplane fly have much to tell scientists about aerodynamics and flight stability. Scientists can study to solve flow problem over the paper airplane. The study can reveal about what makes a good paper airplane, and especially what is needed for smooth gliding. These studies could influence the development of airborne vehicles like drones. Stunt paper airplane seems to have promising advantage, which are very crucial for the paper airplane especially during hovering operation, take-off, and landing manoeuvre.

Author Bio

Prof. R V M. Chokkalingam

Prof. RVM. Chokkalingam is a former lecturer/ curator/scientist, and now @ 80 is a local professor living in Bangalore. He is a SCIENCE MUSEUM SCHOLAR with a specialised curatorial training @ LONDON SCIENCE MUSEUM with specialization in the DESIGN OF SCIENCE EXHIBITS. He has lifetime contribution towards PUBLIC

ENGAGEMENT WITH SCIENCE for over 50 years. He is the recipient of Karnataka State Award for SCIENCE COMMUNICATION in the year 2012. He has published more than 160 ARTICLES in newspapers, magazines, and special publications. He has authored more than 24 BOOKS so far in science, philosophy, nature, and science activity. He is a paper airplane aficionado with lifelong persuasion for origami folding of paper airplanes.

Printed by Libri Plureos GmbH in Hamburg,
Germany